The Night of the Tribades

WORKS BY PER OLOV ENQUIST

Kristallögat, 1961

Färdvägen, 1963

Magnetisörens femte vinter, 1964

Hess, 1966

Sextiotals Kritik, 1966

Legionärerna, 1968 [*The Legionnaires*, trans. Alan Blair]

Sekonden, 1971

Katedralen i München, 1972

Berättelser från de inställda upprorens tid, 1974

Tribadernas natt, 1975

THE
NIGHT
OF THE
TRIBADES

A PLAY FROM 1889

PER OLOV ENQUIST

TRANSLATED FROM THE SWEDISH BY
ROSS SHIDELER

A Mermaid Dramabook

 HILL AND WANG NEW YORK
A division of Farrar, Straus and Giroux

First published in Swedish as *Tribadernas natt,* © 1975 by Per Olov Enquist
English translation © 1977 by Ross Shideler
All rights reserved
Published simultaneously in Canada
by McGraw-Hill Ryerson Ltd., Toronto
Printed in the United States of America
Designed by Karen Watt
First edition, 1977

Library of Congress Cataloging in Publication Data
Enquist, Per Olov. The night of the tribades (A Mermaid dramabook) Translation of Tribadernas natt. 1. Strindberg, August, 1849–1912, in fiction, drama,
poetry, etc. I. Title.
PT9876.15.N78T713   839.7'2'74   77–24982

CONTENTS

--✧ INTRODUCTION ✧--

PER OLOV ENQUIST is recognized throughout Northern Europe as one of the most important and diversified Scandinavian writers of the past twenty years. Since 1961 he has written six novels and two collections of short stories, edited a collection of criticism, and worked as an important and controversial columnist and critic for the liberal Stockholm evening newspaper *Expressen.*

The Night of the Tribades is Enquist's first play, but it reflects the techniques and themes of his earlier writing. A piece of "documentary theater," the play is based on the writings and letters of August Strindberg, yet it goes beyond the specifics of his life. Strindberg's language and psychological fixations, presented within the context of the opening of his play *The Stronger* in Copenhagen in 1889, are brought into the focus of our own time and its socio-political realities. The intense contrast between past and present, the attempt to relate history to modern life, runs as a central theme throughout all of Enquist's writing.

One of his earlier novels, *Magnetisörens femte vinter* (The Magnetizer's Fifth Winter, 1964), is based in part on the life of Mesmer. Both this novel and a later one, *Legionärerna,* 1968 (*The Legionnaires,* 1973), have been translated into more than ten languages. *The Legionnaires,* a documentary novel, deals with the deportation from Sweden of a number of Latvians and Estonians who were drafted into the German army near the end of the Second World War and were then taken prisoners of war by the Swedes when they fled from the oncoming Russians to Sweden. Deportation from Sweden could have meant execution by the Russians, so the event created a great political debate in Sweden in 1945. When the novel was published more than twenty years later, in 1968, it set off a new political debate. Its brilliance and power established it as one of the classic documentary novels of Swedish literature.

A later novel by Enquist, *Sekonden* (The Second, 1971), focuses on sports. It tells the story of a champion hammer-thrower who is exposed as a cheater. The athlete's son narrates the story as he gradually solves the puzzle of why his father betrayed the thing he most loved. The father's fraud reinforces the son's sense of alienation, and the narration is part of the son's effort to regain his ability to love and to trust, by understanding what happened to his father and to him. In *Sekonden,* Enquist suggests that man's willingness to share, to give and to receive freely, is a means of transcending individual bitterness and isolation. Politically, it is socialism that brings about such a sense of unity. In Enquist's work, individual love and social love combine; modern alienation is, presumably, a lack of both.

This balance of political and personal life took on new dimensions in the works written after *Sekonden*. *Katedralen i München* (The Cathedral in Munich, 1972) originated in a series of articles Enquist wrote as a reporter for the 1972 Olympics. Revealing his poignant, subjective sensitivity, these essays explore the economic and political foundations that define the scope and nature of the modern Olympic games. The interviews with individual athletes, and with once famous athletes who are now publicity agents for firms that sell sports equipment, poke fun at commercialism or somberly lay bare the political complexities within the games. In one of these essays, Enquist presents a painful and bitter perspective on the Israeli athletes killed in the attempt to rescue them from their guerrilla captors. This collection was highly praised in Sweden and it further established Enquist as a major young writer.

On the strength of his works and reputation, Enquist was offered in 1973 a five-month appointment by the American Scandinavian Foundation as Thord Grey Professor at the University of California in Los Angeles. Two works resulted from this stay in Los Angeles. The first, *Berättelser från de inställda upprorens tid* (Stories from the Suspended Revolution), appeared in 1974; the second, *Tribadernas natt,* in 1975. All the stories in *Berättelser från de inställda upprorens tid* take place in Southern California, except for one set in West Berlin. Some are based on articles written for *Expressen*.

They present characters who are confused, alienated, or in the process of a complete mental breakdown. With a light and at times almost comic tone, Enquist reveals a world of average people whose misplaced sense of individualism prevents them from seeing the cause of their frustrations. An American Vietnam veteran, who would willingly shoot any Communist on the spot to show his loyalty to the American tradition of freedom, lives in a van parked on the street; he is trying to save enough money to emigrate to Australia. A father whose son was killed in Vietnam finds himself incapable of accepting the young surfers on the beach, and equally incapable of leaving the city where his son is buried.

The sense of inexplicable alienation is one of Enquist's central themes. *The Night of the Tribades* offers no clear resolution, but powerfully depicts the effects of a lack of meaning in life. In his notes for the Stockholm première, Enquist wrote that the play was begun in Los Angeles in the spring of 1973 while he was rereading Strindberg for the classes he was teaching at UCLA. He found himself trying to hide or disguise his famous countryman's conservative and bizarre ideas about women; yet, partially through discussions with his American students, Enquist came to understand that Strindberg's frustration with marriage, his bitterness toward an institution that exploited the man and made a parasite of the woman, and his hatred of women, were not really different from the feelings experienced by many people in the 1970's.

Enquist compares the tendency toward isolation, hatred, and fear in the Strindberg of 1889 with similar tendencies found in America in 1973. Enquist suggests the possibility that the age of industrialism offered too much for a few instead of enough for the many. As a result, people have come to feel unnecessary, unwanted, useless. And it is this sense of "uselessness" that each of the main characters in *The Night of the Tribades* faces.

In Sweden, the debate concerning the play has centered on whether or not it is a "realistic" portrayal of Strindberg. This question is of lesser interest to Americans. What concerns us is the reality of the characters and the significance of their conflict.

The three main characters in the play live in an age of transition, just as we do, and they find themselves caught in a web of historically defined roles. Strindberg's masculinity is the most obvious role; to protect it, he "measures" himself, in the most literal terms, in order to certify mathematically his manhood, his right to a central position among women. When he is no longer in the center, professionally, psychologically, or physically, he feels lost.

Siri von Essen, Strindberg's estranged wife, struggles to free herself from the limited identity of wife and mother. She was an actress before she was burdened with husband and home, and she wants to return to that profession. Strindberg's play *The Stronger* may be her last chance to regain recognition as an actress.

Marie Caroline David, regarded by Strindberg as an alcoholic lesbian, seems to accept herself as a human being and to be willing to accept others as such. However, she can be easily dismissed by Strindberg, and society, by having her identity reduced to the two socially unacceptable labels: alcoholic and lesbian. Through her, we realize that the play *The Stronger* is a reflection of a wish, a kind of magical incantation, produced by Strindberg in the hope of regaining his wife.

Enquist's "documentary" presentation of August Strindberg is realistic in a number of ways. The play refers to a number of real events and real people in the life of Strindberg, and perhaps more remarkable, it uses Strindberg's own writings as a primary source. The profane and explosive style of the play is Strindberg's as much as it is Enquist's. In addition to actual scenes from *The Stronger,* some of the play's speeches are taken verbatim, or partially revised, from Strindberg's letters and from his *A Madman's Defense.* By using actual documents, Enquist reinforces his thesis that the issues and problems of Strindberg's life and times correspond with amazing accuracy to our own. Enquist has changed some facts and reinterpreted events to create his own powerful drama. But the strength of the comparison between 1889 and the 1970's lies in the successful combination of Enquist's personal vision and the reality of the degrading limitations placed on the men and women of both eras.

Not only specific details and words but the general historical framework presented in *The Night of the Tribades* is true. Strindberg was financially insecure most of his life, and obsessed with the need to earn money. Domestically, he seems to have sought the ideal dependent wife, yet three times ended up marrying ambitious young women whom he then saw as rivals.

In 1889, Strindberg was only forty, near the end of his first and longest marriage, and he had already written, among many other works, the historical verse play *Master Olof* (1876); the first realistic Swedish novel, *The Red Room* (1879); and a number of stories about marriage and family life (*Getting Married*, Part I, 1884, and *Getting Married*, Part II, 1885), for which he was taken to court on charges of blasphemy but acquitted. Both collections of stories were written while Strindberg was living abroad, mostly in Switzerland and France. He returned to Sweden for his trial, and this ordeal enraged him.

During the 1880's, Strindberg was fully engaged in the battle of the sexes that was being debated throughout Europe. One of his stories is, in fact, a reply to Ibsen's *A Doll's House* (1879). Obviously, the source of the stories was Strindberg's own marriage and his growing feelings of persecution. While living in an artists' colony in Grez, France (near Fontainebleau), Strindberg made some of his most virulent accusations of infidelity, with both men and women, against Siri. The final collapse of their marriage began during this time. Nevertheless, Strindberg's letters sometimes describe his life in Grez as idyllic, even with Marie Caroline David and her friends visiting him and Siri. Marie was a young Danish girl, an alcoholic, purportedly a lesbian, and associated with the feminists of the time. Strindberg, it seems, could love Siri and enjoy women like Marie, yet bear an abstract hatred toward all women. Strindberg's misogyny is clear in the writings of this period: it was his general feeling that the struggle for women's rights was a demand for equal rights without equal responsibilities.

The plays *The Father* (1887) and *Miss Julie* (1888) reflect not only the battle of the sexes but Darwin's theory of the survival of the fittest and the naturalist movement of Emile Zola. In 1888, Strindberg went to Denmark to create a Scandinavian "experimental theater" patterned after Antoine's Théâtre Libre, established in Paris in 1877. This new "theater" was intended to revolutionize both the subject matter and the form of drama. Unfortunately, *Miss Julie* was censored in Denmark and could be performed only in private in a student production in Copenhagen sponsored by Georg Brandes.

The great Danish critic Brandes encouraged Strindberg's work, and it was partially because of Brandes that Strindberg had gone to Copenhagen. Once there, however, Strindberg became embroiled in a mass of financial and theatrical complications. He tried to get help from different people and in different places, each time with new hope, only to meet with failure. Yet his attempt to succeed in Denmark was more important than ever, since he was at a low point in his professional life in Sweden.

Finally, he was forced to establish his own theater in Copenhagen, using amateur actors, something which had been successfully done in France and England. Strindberg could then experiment, could have his own works performed, and might perhaps save his marriage, by giving Siri a chance to return to the acting career she had given up in the early years of their marriage.

He wrote a number of plays for this theater, all of them calling for a small cast and with minimal stage requirements. Three of them, *The Stronger, Creditors,* and *Paria,* were presented for the first time on March 9, 1889. Lack of money prevented the performance of other works, and the theater was obviously doomed.

On his return to Sweden after the failure of his experimental theater in Copenhagen, Strindberg divorced Siri. He was deeply grieved that he did not get custody of their three children. In 1892 he moved to Germany and there met a young Austrian woman, whom he married. The marriage lasted less than a year. He then went to Paris, where he suffered a severe emotional crisis. It was after this two-year period that Strindberg wrote some of his greatest works, such as *The Dream*

Play and the chamber plays *The Ghost Sonata, The Dance of Death,* and *Storm.*

In the original production of *The Stronger,* the play that Enquist uses as a focus to bring his three main characters together, Siri von Essen-Strindberg played the role of the woman who speaks. Probably, however, the mute role was written for her. *The Stronger* depicts a meeting between two women in a small teashop. Only one of them speaks, while the other listens, reacting in silence. Which woman is actually the stronger is a subject for debate. Both are in love with the same man, and this is the final confrontation between the two women. The monologue is spoken by the wife, Mrs. X, who does not know, when she begins talking, that her husband has had an affair with the other woman, Miss Y. As the one-sided conversation progresses, the wife realizes not only that there has been an affair but that she herself has been remade in Miss Y's image. Her clothes, her taste in food and drink, all have come to her from this woman who now sits facing her. If keeping her husband means victory, then Mrs. X is victorious. But in the process of discovering the affair, she reveals how weak and insensitive she has been.

This is the play that Enquist's characters are preparing to rehearse when *The Night of the Tribades* begins. It is a stroke of genius to put Marie Caroline David in the role of the mute Miss Y. Using the device of a rehearsal to explore Strindberg's motives for writing *The Stronger,* Enquist suggests the possibility that Strindberg wanted to be loved by both women. Perhaps some kind of secret love for each other underlies the conflict between Strindberg and Marie. The truth behind the writing of *The Stronger* must, of course, remain unknown. Yet Strindberg's loss of his wife in real life—Siri moved in with Marie after the divorce—with the love, in the play, of the two women for one man suggests that Strindberg may have been dramatizing a personal fantasy. In any case, *The Stronger* may well be seen in light of *The Night of the Tribades* from now on.

The importance of Enquist's play may be judged in part by its success. Within one year of its première in Stockholm (September 27, 1975), it had been translated into more than seventeen languages and had been performed in nearly every major European country. Its enthusiastic critical reception ranks it as one of the finest plays written in Scandinavia in the past fifty years.

In response to Emile Zola's call for a literature and a theater that could be used as a tool for social reform, Antoine established his Théâtre Libre. Strindberg, in spite of some of his views, was also a great reformer, and his plays document the social causes of personal misery, and the need for social reform. Per Olov Enquist continues this tradition, and it is fitting that Strindberg's attempt to revolutionize Scandinavian theater should serve as an example, if at times a painful one, for this major new artist from Sweden.

P. O. Enquist has cooperated fully in this translation of his play, and variations from the original Swedish have been approved by him. The first production of the play in the United States took place in December 1976, under the direction of Michael Kahn at the McCarter Theatre in Princeton, New Jersey. The fine cast of that production helped me to smooth out the play's unique mixture of Enquist's own modern language and Strindberg's colloquial and associative style. Naturally, final responsibility for the translation is my own.

The UCLA Academic Senate and the Swedish Information Service have either directly or indirectly aided me in this project. Bridget Aschenberg, the play's agent from ICM in New York City, has been of inestimable value in bringing this play to the public.

Ross Shideler

The Night of the Tribades was given its American première
at the McCarter Theatre in Princeton, New Jersey, on December 5, 1976,
with the following cast:

SIRI VON ESSEN-STRINDBERG / *Patricia Elliott*

AUGUST STRINDBERG / *Donald Madden*

VIGGO SCHIWE / *Ted Graeber*

MARIE CAROLINE DAVID / *Kathryn Walker*

PHOTOGRAPHER / *Lawrence Holofcener*

The Night of the Tribades

CHARACTERS

Siri von Essen-Strindberg

Viggo Schiwe

Marie Caroline David

August Strindberg

Photographer

The music is from the late 1800's. It is heavy without being pompous. It rolls forth as the lights go down and continues. The curtain, however, does not go up.

Projections. The curtain is a screen, and pictures begin to appear on it. First, only pictures of faces. They are all men. It is nineteenth-century man who is presented. He looks masculine. He resembles us strikingly, looks quite contemporary, full of vitality. Men with iron jaws. Men who look straight into the future. Men who are uniformly dressed. The pictures become livelier. The men are shown now in various contexts. They ride. They travel on expeditions. They let themselves be immortalized for future generations. They stretch out nets. They kill. They invent machines as well as drive them. They laugh as if hearing good news. They drink together. They screw women.

The description of the man becomes more detailed and factual. A foot with the measurements written beside it. An arm. A diagrammed muscle with the nerves exposed. A body: front view, side view. A detailed drawing of a horizontal penis, also with measurements and proportions (the drawing large and in appearance noticeably like a ship). Machines at work. A rifle design. A spade. A steam engine. A locomotive. Suddenly animals: lions, running dogs, elephants. Natives with muscular bodies. A battle. A savage. A spear. Then the faces.

The faces. They present nineteenth-century man. Finally, only one man. It is August Strindberg. He looks like a young girl
He is afraid.

Music. Swells, and expands. When the curtain goes up, the music sinks slowly aside, very slowly. Very slowly: light.

The scene. It is trashy. It seems, when it now bravely emerges from the darkness, to be somewhat cluttered. On the right, stacked beer crates. However, it is clear that this is not a beer warehouse but, rather, a theater. The stage is cluttered with stage flats. The last play shown here, at the Dagmar Theater in Copenhagen, seems to have been an adventure play in some exotic milieu. Two badly drawn cardboard flats depict the attack of roaring lions. An elephant. Six crudely drawn natives, obviously cannibals on some South Sea island, rush forward with raised spears. A ladder leans against the wall. Several torn advertisements for theater presentations. Two palms in a pot. A somewhat disordered and dreary bourgeois interior: a mahogany desk, two chairs and several pictures of the royal family. A huge bed with a thick, sensuous, red bedspread. On the bed, inexplicably, a chamber pot, two washbasins, and a water pitcher.

The woman is rather tall, between thirty-five and forty, a little bony, has her blond hair done up in a bun. She is cleaning energetically but aimlessly. She tries to move the heavy double bed to the side, but cannot budge it. She takes the chamber pot and the basins from the bed, tries again. It still won't move.

SIRI
(*Swears in a well-mannered voice in a language that sounds like Finnish, tries again, gives up, looks at the bed*) Alla my vossiha rata . . . damned ruppido allat minna . . . terve sakussat . . . umekassat . . . (*Stands still and bursts out*) perkele usti nakasat . . .

STRINDBERG
(*He nearly sneaks in, his clothes give a worn impression, he*

listens with growing delight to her words) Swearwords! Don't deny it! Vulgar Finnish swearwords!

SIRI

(*Looks up abruptly, embarrassed and at the same time irritated*) You're bluffing, August! You don't know anything about Finnish.

STRINDBERG

(*Walks a polite circle around her, looks at her critically*) Swearing in Finnish! The new directress of the new Strindberg Theater in Copenhagen . . . charming woman . . . carries chamber pots and swears like a Finnish peasant . . . yes, yes. When did the rehearsal begin today?

SIRI

(*Has collected her wits*) Well, little August, still alive. Coming all by himself to the Dagmar Theater. How fashionable . . . and besides . . . he *speaks* to me. Will wonders never stop.

STRINDBERG

Cease.

SIRI

What do you mean?

STRINDBERG

Cease, cease. It's a cliché. "Will wonders never cease!" You've begun to get sloppy with your language again. Can't do that if you are going to build a career! And support yourself.

SIRI

(*Very proper*) A half hour ago.

STRINDBERG

A half hour ago?

SIRI

Perhaps I heard incorrectly . . . wait . . . (*Trying to remember*)

Didn't you just ask . . . when the rehearsal began? Yes, I'm certain you did. The answer: the rehearsal today will begin a half hour ago.

STRINDBERG
(*Thrown off-balance somewhat*) Oh yes. Yes? (*Regains control*) But what do I see . . . no one here rehearsing . . . it's empty?

SIRI
(*Amiably*) That's right! You really aren't stupid!

STRINDBERG
Yes, yes? And?

SIRI
It was delayed for an hour. Since you wrote your little note saying that you wished to see the evening rehearsal. We changed the time! By mutual agreement, you might say!

STRINDBERG
(*Glares accusingly at the beer crates*) Did you guzzle all that?

SIRI
Obviously!

STRINDBERG
What the hell are they standing there for? What? Ten crates at least . . . and with your beer thirst . . . Very peculiar.

SIRI
Because, my friend, this theater is used as a warehouse by a brewery when nothing is on! And here, by god, plays do not get performed very often. But the crates soon will be taken away, for Strindberg is coming!

STRINDBERG
(*Restless and nervous*) Yes, yes. When are they coming?

SIRI

No idea! But the beer is certain to be taken away!

STRINDBERG

I mean the actors, damn it; there is going to be a rehearsal here tonight?

SIRI

Quite soon.

STRINDBERG

(*Suddenly anxious*) Siri. There is one thing I must speak with you about before anyone comes. You know . . . privately, between us . . . family problems and private concerns should be kept in the family. (*Gestures convincingly*) That has *always* been my principle.

SIRI

Oh. That's new.

STRINDBERG

New?

SIRI

I thought you earned your daily bread by respectably shoveling together all the private shit about us you could find and publishing it in book form . . .

STRINDBERG

(*Shouts*) But that is art! Literature!

SIRI

Oh, art . . . excuse me, then . . .

STRINDBERG

You know . . . it's Hansen again. That damned gypsy who wants to kill me because I reported him to the police. They say that he is after me again. He intends to reopen the case . . . concerning Martha. You know. He won't give up. It is . . . it is . . . distasteful.

SIRI
Certainly.

STRINDBERG
I must speak with you before . . .

SIRI
Oh, I am so happy.

STRINDBERG
Happy!?

SIRI
(*With great benevolence*) Yes, I know—we are getting a divorce. But I am so happy that you will talk to little me, anyway. Last week when we accidentally met in the dining room of the hotel . . . you sat and ate dinner, if I am not wrong . . . with some pale spiritual admirer . . .

STRINDBERG
My Danish translator!!!

SIRI
The way he hung on your lips, I was afraid you wouldn't be able to get food between them. In any case, I went through the dining room, by mistake. And greeted the Great One! Without having asked for permission! But no: the Great One would not even say hello. You only glared at me as if I were a goddamned rat. Or a pair of old shoes.

STRINDBERG
(*Sadly*) Now you swore again.

SIRI

I felt like a sakutumusset satanas koisternusset valmit markussal. Which you, with your limited language ability, can think about for a while.

STRINDBERG

(*Suspiciously*) That . . . that was not Finnish! You were too *good* to learn Finnish. The Swedish nobility doesn't learn Finnish. You're bluffing!

SIRI

Like a pair of old shoes, then!

STRINDBERG

(*With great weight, wandering around her, hands behind his back, looking up at the ceiling*) They say now that I have rejected you. They say now that I have accepted the consequences of your many lapses and mistakes. I say: they are right. What has happened is necessary. It is a concrete fact. I have, to use a concrete word, rejected you. You are an ex-wife. We can have an open relationship . . . (*Increasingly trustworthy and convincing*) You may be my mistress. However, you are rejected. I do not intend to take you with me to social affairs. Our relationship is purely a business one. The theater. The children. That's all.

SIRI

(*Amazed and moved*) Jesus, what an after-dinner speech . . .

STRINDBERG

But since you are the directress of my newly created Strindberg Theater . . . *designated by me!* . . . I expect . . . not inhumanly or unreasonably . . . that regular hours be kept. Rehearsals should be started! And completed! Accounts should be kept. Someone who is going to support herself and be a free woman cannot be lazy!

SIRI

As far as the Martha case goes, anyway, you don't have to be afraid.

STRINDBERG

(*Nervously*) What? What do you know? What is happening?

SIRI

I mean, what did you really expect? First you begin a dashing affair with an under-age girl. Very charming. Then you begin to feel nervous about her . . . dark-complexioned older brother. Report him on the *weakest* of evidence for theft. Police arrive, throw him in jail. Strindberg happy and eased. The complaint proves to be false. The brother out after a week on bread and water, furious, naturally . . . falsely accused . . .

STRINDBERG

(*Very distinctly*) However, I was completely . . . completely! . . . protected legally! The girl was *not* under-age! Legal! Did it of her own free will! And besides, the brother is a gypsy.

SIRI

Good. Fine. Anyway, he gets out of jail, mad enough to shit on the devil, and wants to kill you. Drinks heavily one night, tries to get into our house, right through the wall, screaming and beating with a hammer. Whereupon you heroically disappear like smoke and I am left to take care of drunk gypsy, defiled sister, and the whole mess, to avoid a trial. And jail.

STRINDBERG

(*In a low voice*) You know I have claustrophobia. I cannot even think of a prison. Every time I try to imagine one . . . a cell . . . I die a little bit. (*Loudly*) Besides, you realized, you damned bitch, that I couldn't earn money if I went to jail!!!

SIRI

I don't give a damn about your affair with the girl. I am not jealous. Besides, I have spoken with the police. Several times. The case is closed.

STRINDBERG

Are you sure?

SIRI

Yes, I'm sure, dear little August.

STRINDBERG

(*Sits, staring emptily straight ahead*) Yes, yes, yes, yes. You are so terrifyingly . . . irrationally . . . strong. Yes, yes. Strong you are. (*Pause*) Thank you. You settled that with an . . . awesome . . . strength. It was shabby, disgustingly shabby. I was so afraid, so terribly afraid.

SIRI

Why didn't you write about *that*, then? Instead of writing that awful and ridiculous story *Tschandala*, in which you slandered and abused gypsies?

STRINDBERG

Because!—if I had written the truth—that I was afraid! god-damned totally afraid! and ran away! and really did not want to screw that little bitch!—everyone would think that I acted like a helpless little old lady (*calmly and matter-of-factly*), and not like a man.

SIRI

Oh, ohhh, sure.

STRINDBERG

Besides, my studies of the female psyche have gotten me interested in criminal psychology. You know . . . women have a criminal nature, too . . . It all fits together. Should be studied.

SIRI
(*Stares quietly at him*) The gangster should be here soon, at that.

STRINDBERG
(*Horrified*) Who? The gangster? Is he coming here? Is that gypsy . . .

SIRI
(*Angelically*) No . . . I only meant the other actress . . . one of those criminal natures you spoke of . . . I thought . . .

STRINDBERG
(*Stiffly*) A truly *bad* joke.

SCHIWE
(*Makes a charm-filled entrance, throws off his raincoat, steps gracefully, opening his arms to Siri and smiling enticingly*) The delightful theater directress Essen-Strindberg! On stage before anyone else! A delicate flower in the theater's rich garden! Siri! (*Walks toward her with outstretched arms, is stopped by her warning look*) Yes? (*Sees* STRINDBERG, *changes his course tentatively toward him, still with open arms, stops somewhat sheepishly and turns his hands aimlessly*)

STRINDBERG
(*Very coldly*) Who the hell is that?

SIRI
Yes, perhaps I should introduce you . . . This is August Strindberg . . . and this is . . .

SCHIWE
(*Effusively, making a gallant and well-considered new beginning*) Mr. Strindberg! I do not believe my eyes! Is it Strindberg himself? Yes, it *must* be you! It is you! I am right! Yes! Then let me beg humbly to present myself, since I now have the honor for the first time of personally (*his speech becoming more formal*

and stereotyped) making the acquaintance of one of the greatest writers of our age—he who, with the suffering of truth, with clarity and daring, has written words that have burned through our very *skin* . . . if I may say so. I have long admired you from afar. And loved you. But now that the Dagmar Theater in Copenhagen has the privilege of having you as a guest, it is a historic . . .

STRINDBERG

(*Stiffly, but flattered*) Oh, please, please. Thank you, thank you.

SCHIWE

(*Now enthralled by the splendor of his own speech*) If I could only show you our devotion! If I could give you my heart! If I had words to describe . . . if I could give you . . .

STRINDBERG

Cash.

SCHIWE

Pardon?

STRINDBERG

Cash. If you want to give me something, give cash.

SCHIWE

Ah, yes . . . ?

STRINDBERG

I'm broke. Therefore, cash. Even small amounts would be accepted.

SIRI

(*Quickly*) And this is the star actor Viggo Schiwe, who as you know rehearsed as Jean in *Miss Julie* . . . and is going to help with the staging and produc . . .

SCHIWE

Viggo Schiwe! One of your warmest admirers!

STRINDBERG

Yes, oh yes! (*Bitterly*) I have heard of you.

SCHIWE

(*Overwhelmingly flattered*) You have heard of me? Is it true?
You, Mr. Strindberg? I should . . . yes. Yes, I know that people
more and more begin to consider me one of Denmark's foremost
actors . . . (*Pause*) perhaps *the* foremost . . . but that you, Mr.
Strindberg . . .

STRINDBERG

(*Coldly*) I have heard *gossip* about you. And Siri.

SCHIWE

(*Somewhat less securely*) Gossip . . . ?

STRINDBERG

As you well know, Siri and I are getting divorced. You have
assumed, therefore, that you can screw around with her without
any risk. Well, you can freeze your balls in hell! This is a theater
and not a whorehouse. Once you have gotten that clear, you can
devote yourself exclusively to keeping your mouth shut!

SCHIWE

(*Indignant*) Mr. Strindberg! (*From the diaphragm*) Mrs. Essen-
Strindberg is a person for whom I have the deepest, the deepest
respect and regard . . .

STRINDBERG

(*Shouting*) Good, keep it that way!

SCHIWE

(*Scared, and suddenly ingratiating*) . . . and shall certainly keep
it that way . . .

STRINDBERG
Concerning *Miss Julie* . . . I have ceased to be amazed by anything.

SCHIWE
Oh?

STRINDBERG
That it was stopped.

SCHIWE
(*Dreamily*) I was very fond of Jean's role during rehearsals. I found that it had a depth, a quality that . . .

STRINDBERG
An old woman of a prosecutor named Mr. Meyer found it immoral and censored it. I could cut the play and try to get it through. That would make hash of it, but who gives a damn, we do it to earn money. However, we don't have time. So we choose something else. *The Stronger*.

SCHIWE
To cut that text would be an outrage . . . it would be a crime.

STRINDBERG
Mr. Schiwe! I am a moneymaking machine! I am forced to produce texts like a machine in order to support parasite women and under-age children. Women *demand* blood and money! Therefore, I cannot *afford* to have the same sentimental view of my work as you do, young man.

SIRI
(*Mildly*) But they are immortal masterpieces, after all?

STRINDBERG
Yes, actually! In spite of everything!

MARIE

(*She comes on stage quietly, nearly unnoticed, stops, listens. She is perhaps twenty-five years old, with short red hair, a soft round face.* STRINDBERG *sees her first. He stiffens as if thunderstruck. Takes a step toward her, stops. It is absolutely quiet.* SCHIWE *understands nothing.* SIRI *looks afraid.* MARIE *looks calmly at* STRINDberg, *but one sees that she is tense*) Forgive me, I am late.

STRINDBERG

(*Spins around, goes abruptly up to* SIRI) What does this mean?

SIRI

You don't know?

STRINDBERG

Don't know what?

SIRI

There is a mute role in *The Stronger.* Marie was kind enough to offer to play it.

STRINDBERG

(*Slowly, softly to* SIRI) Soooo, your little friend appears again.

SIRI

As you see.

STRINDBERG

(*Thoughtfully*) The repulsive little Danish tribade. Aha, then I should have killed her right there in Grez three years ago. It wasn't enough just to throw her out.

SIRI

(*Softly*) I am free now. You must accept it. That's the way it is.

STRINDBERG

Was it you who took . . . the initiative?

SIRI

That's none of your business.

STRINDBERG

Isn't it?

SIRI

It's none of your business.

SCHIWE

Miss David has . . . in spite of her lack of theatrical experience
. . . demonstrated a rich, sincere, and charming range of facial
expressions which persuades me that . . .

STRINDBERG

Do you *know* Miss David?

SCHIWE

No more than as a charming . . .

STRINDBERG

So you do not know her. (*Pause*) But I do.

SCHIWE

Have you . . . met before . . .

STRINDBERG

Unhappily. But a year ago there was a rumor that she drank
herself to death. Unfortunately, it wasn't true.

SCHIWE

But you shouldn't . . .

STRINDBERG

(*Explosively, glaring threateningly at* SCHIWE) I dislike *everyone*
who fawns over my wife! Is that understood!??

MARIE

I am here now. It can't be changed. I haven't forgotten what happened, but I don't care about it. We must try to stick to the point.

STRINDBERG

(*Rouses himself, walks to a chair, grabs it, slams it down with a bang, and, looking directly at* MARIE, *points a finger shaking with anger at the seat of the chair*) There! There! Precisely there is where Miss David should sit during the coming hours! (*Still pointing at the chair, with growing emotion*) And shut up! The newly written play that we are now going to rehearse . . . to carry it toward an inevitably catastrophic première . . . is my own one-act play *The Stronger*. For the debilitated, or for those of us who are perhaps illiterate (*a long look at* SCHIWE), I will add that this *excellent* (*looks threateningly around, no one dares protest*) that this *excellent* play has two roles, one of which is *mute! M* as in man-hating, *u* as in useless, *t* as in tribade, *e* as in evil. Mute! She will therefore sit there. And be mute!

MARIE

(*Shakes her head in resignation, smiles and sits down on the chair*) Siri, my friend. What won't I do for you?

STRINDBERG

(*Pointing, still impassioned*) Will sit there. And continually and with the greatest of will power, as long as it lasts, keep her mouth shut!

MARIE

(*Amiably curious*) What have they done to you, Mr. Strindberg? The first time I met you in Grez you were so gentle, friendly. You are really one of the most gentle, most sensitive, and tender men I know, not at all . . .

STRINDBERG

(*Fighting to stay calm*) And this, she throws this into my face, I must listen to this . . .

MARIE

. . . I mean sensitive, but not at all . . .

STRINDBERG

(*Icy cold*) Bring over the pot, Mr. Schiwe, the woman is beginning to spread her shit.

MARIE

Why this excessive . . . virile . . . volcanic outburst, as if you must pretend . . . as if you are afraid that otherwise you would not be a man . . .

SIRI

Aren't you going to try to be at least polite to Marie? It is so *unbelievably* unforgiving. I mean, we did live together for nearly a year in Grez. As friends.

SCHIWE

(*Painfully, touched*) Perhaps I should withdraw a moment . . .

STRINDBERG

Do what you want. If this is painful, please go. Come back when it is not painful.

SCHIWE

Perhaps for a short while. (*Hovers indecisively on his toes, stays*)

STRINDBERG

Although there is not much that isn't painful. Even to remember . . . (*pause*) is painful. Yet I cannot stop it. I remember this little tribade's departure. Marie Caroline David. Marie Caroline David. Siri as the Queen of the Night. And she as the queen of the tribades. I never thought they would reunite after the night of the tribades in Grez.

SCHIWE

What kind of a night was it . . . (*Stops, embarrassed*)

STRINDBERG

(*Looking thoughtfully at* MARIE) Marie. Caroline. David.

SIRI

(*Briskly*) It is time now! Let's begin! We have delayed long enough; we must begin rehearsing now! I have waited all these years to get back on stage and nothing is going to stop me! Let's get going! Everyone be nice to everyone. August is sitting there watching the girls kindly. We'll begin to rehearse. Then we'll see how far we get!

SCHIWE

(*Eased*) Is it *really* so long since Mrs. Essen-Strindberg was on stage? What a pity. The art of the theater *lost* so much when you gave it up . . .

STRINDBERG

(*Sourly*) Oh, bullshit. The theater survived goddamned well! And art is doing fine, too. But it is true; she married in order to build her career through me. I was in love and dumb; she was hungry for a career. Plain and simple. A charming woman.

SIRI

That, that is rewriting history. God, I'll be damned. Don't forget to add, dear little August, that I was then stuffed into marriage and maid's work, like a cow for seven lean years. That was a career, my friend. Thank you very much.

STRINDBERG

(*Delighted*) Exactly. *All your plans were for nothing!!*

MARIE

You two have said this to each other at least eight times a week for seven years. Don't you have any *new* . . . any original subjects for your fights?

SIRI

Just give me a new, original life, and we'll fix that, too.

MARIE

But what good does it do, to *repeat* all the . . .

STRINDBERG

(*Pointing sadly at* MARIE) She always *forgets* herself. She is supposed to be mute. Look here at the first page. It is written here. Yet still she babbles; sooner or later I am going to lose *patience* with her . . .

SCHIWE

But the facial expressions . . . We must not forget that this mute role is played with the help of miming . . . The face can be shaped into expressive lines . . . can give expression to doubt, to moving . . . intense feelings . . . The hands can also . . . gesture with passion . . . Eyes open wide mean fear . . .

STRINDBERG

(*Looking at him with an expression of absolute dislike*) Siri, my darling ex-wife, you are a charming woman, but you have always had *unbelievably* bad judgment in lovers. Look at this . . . passionate . . . toad. Such unbelievably bad judgment. Merchantmen and stupid lieutenants on the boat to Finland, and blockheaded third-class actors, and lesbian women from Copenhagen. Never anyone I could *respect!* Never.

SIRI

(*Exercising self-control*) Let me point out rather strongly that nothing whatsoever has happened between me and Mr. Schiwe.

STRINDBERG

(*Thoughtfully*) Sometimes I think that you . . . consciously . . . tried to hurt me . . . to reduce me . . . by never taking anyone whom I could *respect*. Never.

SIRI

Oh, my god. What a menagerie I must have plowed my way through. This is . . .

SCHIWE

(*Has puffed himself up until he is full, and now bursts out*)
Now I demand an apology! That is going too far! I demand an
apology and a means of redress! Mr. Strindberg has called me
a toad!

STRINDBERG

(*In amazement*) Oh, but that must be wrong? Surely I said a
passionate toad?

SCHIWE

(*Confused*) Did you say that?

STRINDBERG

Yes, I remember it quite well. You can ask the women.

SIRI

Yes, that is what he said.

STRINDBERG

See there!!

SCHIWE

Yes, hmmmm. (*Thinks intensely*) I demand . . . an apology
anyway!

STRINDBERG

But of course. (*Kind and amicable*) I beg your pardon, Mr.
Schiwe. That was stupid of me. (*Puts his arm around* SCHIWE's
*shoulder and in a mood of camaraderie walks with him slowly
across the stage*) Mr. Schiwe, you are my friend. We must stick
together. *Many* would certainly criticize you . . . call you dumb
. . . or unbelievably stupid . . . unbelievably!!! . . . But I certainly don't say that. I say: you, in spite of everything, are a
man! We have similar interests. Basically, we are both on the
same side in this battle. We must stand united in the fight against
women.

MARIE

Now I really must ask: what's it going to be—a battle against the ladies or a rehearsal. Is there going to be a rehearsal here this evening or not?

SCHIWE

That's true, we must . . .

SIRI

For god's sake, page 1 from the beginning, pay attention now and don't act like . . .

STRINDBERG

. . . like women . . .

SIRI

Page 1 from the beginning.

STRINDBERG

This entirely new one-act play (*more and more energetically and excitedly*) which is finally having its première . . . world première! . . . is a moving description of two women's final confrontation. They both love the same man. They fight over him. He is absent, but dominates the scene anyway. As so often happens. One of the women finally wins the confrontation and returns to the man. The scene is very simple. A corner in a small teashop. Two little iron tables, a red settee, and several chairs. Siri comes in . . . wrong, I mean Mrs. X comes in! Dressed in winter clothes . . . a hat and a coat and a nice Japanese basket on her arm. At one of the tables sits . . . the one we call Miss Y. In my opinion, a very *unappealing* woman (*walks around the stage in small happy turns*), red-haired, with baby fat and a curved nose . . . (*Stops after a warning look from* SIRI) In any case! She sits there in front of a half-empty bottle of beer and reads an illustrated woman's magazine. In a nutshell, her two favorite occupations. A remarkably accurate description. Especially the bottle of beer . . . (*Thoughtfully*) . . . That totally incomprehensible consumption of beer . . . up to twenty a day . . . sometimes more, if I remember correctly, and I do . . .

SIRI
August . . .

STRINDBERG
(*Cheerily*) Yes, yes. So Miss David sits mute, drinks beer, and reads an illustrated magazine, which she later exchanges for others. Illustrated magazines!

SCHIWE
(*Somewhat sulky at being ignored*) A few stage directions might be useful at this point . . . a passionate . . . a powerful inner concentration . . . an artless and pleasant monologue . . . with a warmth which . . .

STRINDBERG
Mr. Schiwe, begin!

SCHIWE
For Miss David's part, perhaps a calm and intense expression would be proper during the introduction . . .

STRINDBERG
What damned jabbering! Begin! Begin!

SIRI
(*Beginning the play*) "Hello, Amelie, my dear. You sit here so alone, on Christmas Eve, like a poor bachelor."

MARIE "*looks up from the newspaper, nods, and continues to read.*"

SIRI
"Do you know that it pains me to see you—alone, alone in a café, and on Christmas Eve. It pains me just as it did once in Paris when I saw a bridal party in a restaurant and the bride

sat and read a book of jokes while the bridegroom played billiards with the witnesses. Oh, I thought, if this is the way they start, how will they go on, and how will they end. He played billiards on their wedding day. And she read a jokebook, you know? Oh well, it is not at all the same."

STRINDBERG

(*Chuckling*) Not at all. Hell, much worse. Here the waitress comes in with a cup of chocolate for the non-beer-drinking woman. Mr. Schiwe, since you played Jean in *Miss Julie* and dominate, as one might say, the *servile,* you can stand in today. Only pretend to serve it. (*Helpfully*) Intense concentration now, Mr. Schiwe, calm and passionate expression, persuasively and expressively!

SCHIWE

(*With insight*) That could be thought of as a subtle little dig!

STRINDBERG

Not subtle, Mr. Schiwe! Not subtle! (*Now joyously on the offensive*) Miss David, I must warn you, must in all friendliness remind you that at the première, it will not be a man who is the waitress. Then a cute young girl will come in! Then Miss David must control her impulses! Don't finger the girl! Don't paw her! Don't touch her breast! No caresses! No suffering looks! It would ruin the *logic* of the play.

MARIE

(*Low and intense*) There are actually limits to how vulgar you get to be, Mr. Strindberg. That is vulgar and weak, and it is low. I won't get into it.

STRINDBERG

(*Happy*) You are hurt! You are going to leave in a rage! Never to return! Is that so!?

SIRI
(*Slaps the script hopelessly on the floor*) Well, that's it. I was waiting for it. So unbelievably typical of him. And just now, now when I'm getting my first chance in years to work professionally, he destroys it. Calmly and quietly.

STRINDBERG
What? What? What have I done?

MARIE
Siri, surely you aren't going to be surprised?

SIRI
Not really. But every time I am just as disappointed.

STRINDBERG
(*A little restless and guilty, wanders over to* SCHIWE) It's hard to work with women. They don't stick to the subject. They get so damned *personal*, for the least little thing. They cannot see the principle of things. You are a man. You understand what I mean. (*Roaring*) *You understand what I mean!*

SCHIWE
(*Unnerved*) Yesss, I understand what . . . (*Seeking some way to save himself*) Perhaps a more impassioned acting style would be proper here . . . with more expressive gestures.

SIRI
Marie. Dear Marie.

STRINDBERG
Page 2 in the middle. The waitress goes out and does not return. The vivisection continues and Mrs. X speaks. Siri, thank you . . .

SIRI
(*To Marie*) I would really like to do this role. I need this chance to work again. I *desperately* want to do it. I do.

STRINDBERG

(*Nearly apologetic*) Page 2 in the middle . . .

MARIE *goes silently to the chair, casts a long look at Strindberg, sits down.*

STRINDBERG

(*To* SCHIWE) See. A completely unnecessary interruption. Luckily, I remained calm.

SIRI

"Do you know what, Amelie? I believe you would have been better off keeping your fiancé. Do you remember that I was the first one to tell you to forgive him? Do you remember that? You could have been married now and had a home. Do you remember last Christmas how happy you were when you were out with your fiancé's family in the country . . ."

SCHIWE

Here perhaps Miss David could make a *melancholy* expression . . .

STRINDBERG

Can we really continue borrowing beer out of those crates like that? Isn't it thievery? Otherwise, black coffee would be good now. Real coffee, not like that damned stuff the maids in Grez used . . . (*Fatherly*) And, Schiwe, don't say such stupidities *so often*. A melancholy expression? Why? Completely absurd, and wrong. Miss . . . Miss Y had a fiancé once, that we know. The poor bastard. He couldn't have had much fun. But then he managed to escape the fox trap, and both he and Miss Y are free. But she does not regret it. She is *happy*. She has those kinds of *tendencies*.

SCHIWE

(*Completely confused*) But, according to the text of the play, she . . .

SIRI

This is incredible.

STRINDBERG

An absent man—preferably a dead man—that is happiness for this miss. (*Secretly, to* SCHIWE) Sometimes she goes to the graveyard, when she is depressed, looks at gravestones, reads the names of dead men to cheer herself up. A name. A name . . . dead enemies. You must look reality in the face, Schiwe. *Such is our opponent!*

SCHIWE

But . . . the play . . . you are so hard to . . . (*Uneasily*) Are you joking, Mr. Strindberg?

MARIE

How are we going to have it now? Is it my life that is to be discussed? Or this play, and this woman, who, according to the *script* anyway, is not identical with me?

STRINDBERG

(*Hopefully*) Black coffee would be terribly good. Think . . . think if Schiwe . . . who once played Jean . . . in *Miss Julie* . . . and . . .

SCHIWE

(*Tired and bitter*) . . . dominates the servile, yes, I know, I'll try. God, nearly an hour has gone by, and if this continues, we won't be through before tomorrow morning. (*Makes coffee*)

SIRI

Before I collapse, I just want one thing clear. This is the way I read the script. Two women who have been separated for a long time meet. They are both in love with the same man. It comes to a contest of wills between them. The stronger wins. She returns to her husband. Right?

STRINDBERG

Absolutely correct! The absent man is the central figure! Both love him, and fight for him! (*Lightly*) In a woman's way.

SIRI

Quite right, my love. That is the script. So, goddamn it, let us keep to the script and not add Marie's ex-fiancé to the recipe.

STRINDBERG
Who is doing that?

SIRI
You!!!

STRINDBERG
Am I???

MARIE

This is a strange play, anyway. It's like reading something that keeps concealing itself. Disguising itself. Everything important exists outside the script. When did you write it?

STRINDBERG
Not long after you . . . left Grez.

MARIE
Oh, then.

STRINDBERG
Exactly, then.

SCHIWE

(*Fiddling with his coffee, curious*) When was it written, did you say?

STRINDBERG

(*Looking thoughtfully at him*) Mr. Schiwe. Schiwe. You must have a first name too?

SCHIWE
Viggo.

STRINDBERG
(*Thoughtfully*) I go. You go. We go. Viggo. (*Distastefully*)
Not a very appealing name. Viggo. (*Controlling himself*) However, you are a man. With a man you can talk. Criminals, apes,
and women—all of them are animals of instinct. But you can talk
with a man. Do you understand?

SIRI
Nod agreeably, so little Strindberg will be happy. It makes no
difference to us.

SCHIWE *is terribly uncomfortable, tries to smile, shakes his head*
dubiously, and looks longingly at the door.

STRINDBERG
(*Factually*) I wrote the play after I threw Miss David and her
equally lesbian friend Sofie out of our respectable home in Grez.
(*Shouts out suddenly, in delight*) Your name! It's the same as a
Swedish children's book. Little Viggo's adventure on Christmas
Eve. Hah! (*Completely calm*) Afterwards, I wrote the play. It's
that simple.

SCHIWE
(*Uncomprehending*) Threw them out? Why?

SIRI
(*Thoroughly resigned*) For god's sake, don't trouble yourself.
Just tell him. Every time I hear you, it is the same bewildering
experience. A few facts, a big fraud.

SCHIWE
But . . . but you didn't physically throw her out? . . . That
would be the least chivalrous thing, Mr. Strindberg . . .

STRINDBERG

You must try to understand. (*Turns toward* SCHIWE, *pleading, closes his eyes intensely*) Mr. Schiwe, you must try to understand my *situation* in those years. To live isolated from everyone and in a *foreign* country is like living in darkness . . . surrounded by all these *dangerous* fluttering female bats. (*Appealing to him*) Mr. Schiwe, you understand, when I say that it feels *dangerous* . . . aren't you afraid too? (*Shouting*) . . . I know that you are *damned* afraid when you spread your sweeping compliments around you like shit! . . . (*Softly*) . . . exactly like bats in the darkness. (*Straightens up, objectively*) In any case: two women friends came from Copenhagen and lived with us in Grez. Marie and Sofie Holten. (*Scornfully*) Little *Ole!*—as the latter was called. Ole! These goddamned man-haters who always dress themselves up in men's names! Both are tribades, lesbians. One is supposed to be literary. The other dabbles in painting. And then, Mr. Schiwe. Then it happens. *Then they take my wife away from me.*

SCHIWE

Yes, Mr. Strindberg.

STRINDBERG

I tolerate them. (*Calmly, patiently*) I live with them. I endure my wife's long declarations of affection to Miss David . . . Charming body . . . breasts. Those . . . caresses . . . I understand nothing. They kiss each other, always walk around together . . . as if I *did not even exist* . . . (*Almost as if childishly wronged*) I don't even get to know what is wrong with me . . . Finally, I don't even think anything is wrong . . . I *do not exist!* The children begin to like her, too. Marie . . . Marie . . . Always the damned harping on Marie. And then the perverse erotic . . . I must *tell* someone about that.

MARIE

Right. We must talk about it. I begin to understand for the first time that it is necessary . . .

SCHIWE

Is it necessary?

STRINDBERG

Why not?

MARIE

It is absolutely necessary.

SIRI

To understand the play we are producing?

STRINDBERG

(*Roaring*) Quit talking bullshit about understanding it; the play is about the absent man, that's all. Shut up, I'm going crazy, now begin!

MARIE

That's right. The lost center.

STRINDBERG

Then that night came. The situation was wild and dangerous. Marie had to leave . . . She had entangled herself!—with a girl from the local farms. And the farmers were angry; she had to leave. (*Nearly desperate*) Presumably, I could have had her put into prison. That kind of thing is punishable! But I let her escape, for my wife's sake, and because . . . And then. At the farewell dinner . . .

SCHIWE

(*Incredulously*) Did you really have a dinner for her, after that?

STRINDBERG

Hell, yes! Naturally a farewell dinner! Weren't we *good friends?* And that night . . . that I remember so well . . . with the

light, mild, delicate night rain that stopped just at dawn . . .
(*Grows silent, hesitates*) It was not difficult to determine that
my dear Siri . . . I am sorry to have to bring you into it . . .
although you deserve it! So I am not ashamed! My dear wife's
burning love for the charming Marie Caroline David.

SCHIWE

Mr. Strindberg! Mr. Strindberg!

STRINDBERG

(*Droning softly, nearly chanting*) It rained almost the entire
night, and finally I went out and stood there alone in the rain.
The window . . . was like a picture. I stood there for a long
time . . . Then I went in. And there they were, together. You
should have seen the object of my wife's *burning* flame. I remember her *clearly*. I can even *see* her. Marie Caroline David, I
see her so well. Red-haired . . . Little rolls of baby fat, and a
curved nose, pudgy chin, and yellow eyes, the cheeks swollen
by drinking . . . She drank constantly . . . Flat breasts and
bony hands . . . The most detestable, the most gruesome kind of
woman one can imagine, a farm boy had run away from her
. . . Pudgy chin . . . yellow eyes . . . Somewhat bloated by all
the alcohol . . . Sagging around the mouth . . . Yellow eyes
. . . swollen cheeks . . .

SCHIWE

(*Incredulously*) Do you mean . . . really . . . Miss David?

STRINDBERG

(*Even more disconsolate, monotonous*) And Siri sang a romantic
song . . . with her rather pretty and delicate voice . . . and
when she was finished . . . she began to cry. Then she sat down
beside the monster, and that Danish monstrosity raised herself,
took my wife's head in her hands, and with open mouth devoured
her lips. At least this love is not platonic, I thought. (*Pause*) And
then it was nearly light outside.

SCHIWE
And what did you do, Mr. Strindberg?

STRINDBERG
I got the swine dead drunk.

SCHIWE
Do, do you . . . mean Mrs. Strindberg?

STRINDBERG
I do not usually call my wife a swine. Unless of course she deserves it. Naturally, I meant Miss David.

MARIE
Thanks.

STRINDBERG
(*Almost lovingly, looking at* MARIE) Then I remember we went out, since you felt sick. And I remember that you fell on your knees, looked at me with your wide, terrified eyes, uttered little hiccuping idiotic cries, and leaned against . . . was it a gatepost? And then it was daylight. You vomited. (*Thoughtfully*) Never, never have I seen anything in human form as monstrous as that.

MARIE
(*Rises, goes to Strindberg, looks at him silently for a long time*) Was that the way you saw it?

STRINDBERG
My opinion of women's emancipation was set from then on.

No one speaks, there is silence.

SCHIWE
(*At last, hesitantly*) Is all that true?

STRINDBERG
Ask the women.

SCHIWE
Is all that true?

SIRI
You understand . . . there are two kinds of authors. One kind lies by putting together small fragments of truth. The other tells the truth with a collection of lies.

STRINDBERG
And which type am I?

SIRI
The worst.

SCHIWE
(*Still shaken*) . . . But what did you do, Mrs. Strindberg? . . . How did you feel? . . .

SIRI
I didn't do anything. I only felt sad.

STRINDBERG
(*Low, almost regretfully, speaking only to her*) Siri had lost her beloved and was restless and unhappy. She walked around in the forest mostly, sang songs and visited her friend's favorite places. She cried, and mourned. Wasn't it that way, Siri?

SIRI
For four years we had lived . . . outcasts in the European desert . . . traveled and lived in *pensions,* and fought . . . I had lived with this terrified child who pretends to be a giant. And there was no use, absolutely no use for the person I could be, might have been. I sat there and waited for better times. And waited. And got older. Then this woman arrives from the Danish city of Copenhagen in Northern Europe. And she is completely free. She talks to me as if I am a truly useful human being. Tells me that *it is not too late!* Oh, dear god, why shouldn't I love her?

SCHIWE

Yes.

SIRI

I can't help it. I felt sad when he threw her out. I liked her.

STRINDBERG *looks quietly at her, dubious, wants to say something, but is silent.*

SIRI

(*Explodes*) And absolutely the only thing this one-eyed shit sees is that this free human being should be a lesbian alcoholic! As if *that* were so unbelievably *important!*

STRINDBERG

(*In amazement*) Yes, but certainly it is worth noting, anyway . . .

SIRI

Good! Note it, then! Have you got your notes ready!?

SCHIWE

I would still like to ask, with Mr. Strindberg, if that is not . . .

SIRI

Perhaps, you see, there is something more important in Marie for me than that.

STRINDBERG

(*To* SCHIWE) I can in confidence tell you that those three fiendish women on the one hand insisted on playing whist every night for one year and on the other hand could never learn the rules of whist. Now do you understand what *suffering* is?

MARIE

You told us one time about your father . . . that you hated his "Icelandic nature" so terribly. You did not want to be like him. Have you changed—what has happened to you?

SIRI

Don't ask him. All that was *lost* a long time ago. When he is not in the *center,* he is terrified; everything falls apart for him, and he is as dangerous as a scared rattlesnake.

STRINDBERG

(*Shocked*) These pathetic and bizarre attempts at digging in my soul . . . which does not *concern* any of you! My soul belongs to literary history, and you should not give a goddamn about it, Siri!

MARIE

May a disgusting red-haired woman with baby fat and a pudgy chin ask you something?

STRINDBERG

But of course.

MARIE

Was it after that night that you decided to write your play about the reunion of the two loving women?

STRINDBERG *is silent.*

MARIE

And this is . . . that?

STRINDBERG *nods.*

MARIE

(*To herself*) I must not have understood much of it.

SIRI

(*With exaggerated humility*) How would it be if we . . . perhaps I might suggest . . . in all humility . . . that we devote a few minutes' work to the rehearsal . . . or . . . ?

STRINDBERG

(*Relieved*) Yes, that's right! Now let us begin! It will be damned fun! Now we will rehearse the tribades' reunion.

SIRI

(*Controlled*) I can imagine what he imagines.

STRINDBERG

Iron-hard work! Enough talk! Strength and feeling! More coffee besides, it wouldn't hurt! Mr. Schiwe, who has played Jean in *Miss Julie* anyway and dominates . . . (*Hesitates before* SCHIWE'S *murderous look*) . . . could perhaps . . . Thank you, Schiwe! Thank you! That's right! Coffee for the men and more beer for the women! Now we can begin!

MARIE

(*Softly, staring at him*) Mr. Strindberg. Now I remember.

STRINDBERG

Yes?

MARIE

I remember *how it was*. Why I liked you so very much. That time. Now I remember.

STRINDBERG

(*Absolutely still, expressionless*) Yes?

Music.

A projection on the curtain. It presents a man with a bird's head.

The stage. First darkness. Then the stage lights slowly. SIRI *sits bent over the script, reading intently.* MARIE *opens a bottle of beer.* STRINDBERG *stands a couple of meters from* SIRI, *looks at her, sways up on his toes, seems to want to say something more, but hesitates.*

STRINDBERG
And the children are well?

SIRI
(*Without looking up*) Yes.

STRINDBERG
(*Hesitantly*) Has Karin learned to use the camera equipment I sent her?

SIRI
(*Abruptly*) Don't know.

STRINDBERG
I could perhaps . . . (*Carefully*) If they could live a few weeks with me in the archipelago this summer, they could . . .

SIRI
No.

STRINDBERG

. . . then you could be free . . .

SIRI

No.

MARIE *sits with a newly opened bottle of beer in her hand, looking melancholically straight ahead.*

STRINDBERG

How would it be if Miss David had a beer perhaps?

MARIE *looks at him without changing expression.*

STRINDBERG

It doesn't taste bad. Try one, just for the sake of tasting it once. Only one . . .

MARIE

Sure, I'll have a beer. Or several. You see, Mr. Strindberg, I have never ever—either in Grez or elsewhere—made any secret of the fact that I am an alcoholic. I am one. I don't try to hide the fact.

STRINDBERG

(*Somewhat taken aback*) Oh! Oh well, then!

MARIE

Exactly.

STRINDBERG

Yes . . . well then, skål!

MARIE

Skål.

STRINDBERG

(*Walks around, gets a hold of himself, straightens up*) In point after point it can be shown . . . in spite of claims of lies and exaggerations . . . that I am right. It can be proven. Now the continuous drinking. Everyone here heard the admission, isn't that true? Schiwe, too, who is a man anyway, and not like women, who habitually lie the truth away? You heard it, too?

MARIE

I can prepare a notarized statement for the author to use in his books. I assume I will appear in them shortly . . .

SIRI

Oh my god, yes!

STRINDBERG

What? What?

SIRI

I can only say, oh my god. That's why he writes so much about female vampires. Talk about vampires: I believe his works are a collection of self-portraits. Mr. Strindberg's cunning little self-criticism. God, what a man-eater he is.

STRINDBERG

A portrayer, a man-portrayer! That is the difference, little woman!

SIRI

(*With a charming dance step*) You see here . . . before your amazed and enchanted eyes . . . the pig of Norse mythology— eaten every night, and alive again the next day . . . eaten and reborn again in at least ten of the master's most well known and appreciated works! Still living! Still willing to be devoured again!

STRINDBERG

(*Aroused*) I have made this pig into an international celebrity! And she does not even have the brains to be grateful!

SIRI

Grateful! To be publicly scandalized and misused? Until I lie there with my bare heart bleeding on the floor!? Grateful??

STRINDBERG

(*Didactically*) Listen. You think you lie there beaten and bleeding. Your heart is naked. You lie there and bleed. Then you must say to yourself: here I lie and make literary history! Hier liege ich und mache Literaturgeschichte!

SIRI

(*Seriously agitated*) You eat people up. You consume them! You should have seen the night poor Victoria tried to commit suicide at the hotel where we were staying. Oh my god. That idiot Lundegård who came rushing in to us afterwards and told us the whole story. That lamb. Besides, a man never can learn to keep his mouth shut. But, dear Jesus, how Mr. Strindberg listened! Ohhhhh! (*She circles around him, imitates a greedy and gorging animal, eyes open wide, tongue licking her lips*) Ohhhhh! What a story to devour! What an expression on the Master's face . . . The interest of a merciless cannibal . . . And what details he stuffed in himself! A young girl who tries to commit suicide! Unhappy love affair! Deserted! Knives, blood, gobble . . . slurp . . . slurp . . . Perhaps material for a play? Slurp! A noble-woman . . . midsummer's eve . . . A story with a man . . . Miss Julie is deserted . . . slurp . . . a razor . . . And how his eyes . . . absolutely cold and exact . . . icily noted and registered every detail . . .

MARIE

But, Siri, why do you say that? . . . You see as well as I do the immense compassion in the play . . . What does the expression on his face have to do with it?

SIRI

You haven't been devoured as often as I have! That's the difference!

STRINDBERG

(*Furious*) And this woman, this marauding traitress, I have been forced to love. Terrible. Terrible.

MARIE

(*Surprised*) But do you really love her?

STRINDBERG

Naturally, I love her, and naturally, I will continue to love her
. . . But surely that's nothing that she should consider a *merit?*
When one loves someone, it's something . . . something that
just comes. Like cancer. Or bubonic plague.

MARIE

Oh yes???

STRINDBERG

(*With great seriousness*) The thing that really irritates me is
that it was *precisely she,* whom I dislike so much, that I happened
to fall in love with.

SCHIWE

Whom you dislike so much?

STRINDBERG

Isn't that an infuriating injustice!!!

SIRI

(*Coldly*) Anyway, you are a vampire.

STRINDBERG

Yes. Probably true. (*Very peacefully*) You are a parasite attached
to me who sucks my blood and money and harasses the maids
and lazily dreams of careers you are not up to. And I am a
vampire sucking your blood. That's a typical family life?

SCHIWE

(*Stunned, to himself*) If only I could understand . . . what it is
really that is supposed to be so remarkable about authors.

SIRI

(*Categorically*) Nothing!!!

STRINDBERG

Yes, I know. We write down words. Basically, that is truly remarkable.

SCHIWE

Is it really?

STRINDBERG

I write down on paper man's feelings and fears before he realizes he has them. A year before—ten years—a hundred years! When you see the words, the feelings, documented, then you get indignant and frightened. Not about women's terrorism against us. Which should be quite natural. But you get indignant at the person who writes the words down! That is what I find remarkable!

SIRI

Do you hear, Marie? Little August has plucked up his courage quite a bit since Grez. What vitality!

MARIE

Think, if all that energy could only be used to fight for women's freedom . . .

STRINDBERG

(*Infuriated, screaming*) *You can stop drooling and dry your cunt,* Miss David!! If you have one!!! (*Controls himself*) Yes, yes, yes. Excuse me. That was stupid. *That was stupid,* I said! I have begged your pardon! Does it have to be in writing??? (*Completely calm, disillusioned*) Besides, dear friends, there we lived in Grez in great friendship and great misery, but how? I was forced, month in and month out, to play whist every night with two Danish lesbians plus a wife who was working hard to become one. *Not one of them bothered to learn the rules of whist.* At night you lie and lick each other. And in the day you suggest that I, bearing these three women of society on my shoulders, should fight for the liberation of women. The answer is no!

SCHIWE
But the rehearsal . . . the rehearsal . . . the play . . . What is going to happen to it?

MARIE
Would you get me another beer, please, Siri?

STRINDBERG
(*Angrily pushing forth the script*) Page 2 at the bottom. Miss David sits quietly on the chair, Siri praises the joys of home. Begin!

SIRI
Where?

STRINDBERG
"There is no place like home."

MARIE
Exactly what my presumably syphilitic father used to say every Wednesday and Friday when he came out of the bedroom after raping my mother.

STRINDBERG
There is no place like home!

SIRI
"Yes, dear Amelie, there is no place like home—and next is the theater—and the children, you see—yes, but you don't understand that."

STRINDBERG
No, that sounds like hell. (*Pleading*) You must be convincing, Siri. You are talking to an emancipated ape who has deserted everything, who only goes around saying a lot of crap about

freedom. You have the upper hand! Be convincing! You must convince!! (*Aroused, to* SCHIWE) It's significant that there is not one woman in history who could sell horses! They have no convincing spark, *no fire!*

SIRI

Yes, dear. "(*Opens the basket and shows the Christmas presents*) Here, you can see what I bought for my little darlings. (*Lifts out a doll*) Do you see this one? This is Lisa's. Do you see how she rolls her eyes and turns her head! Oh, oh, here is Maja's cork pistol. (*Loads it and fires at Y*)"

MARIE *giggles, amused.*

SCHIWE

(*Worried*) Here perhaps it would be appropriate to have a more flexible and expressive face that . . .

STRINDBERG

She is supposed to look afraid!!!

MARIE *with an exaggerated look of terror.*

STRINDBERG

(*Giving up*) Oh my god, what a performance this is going to be.

SIRI

"Were you afraid? (*Takes out a pair of embroidered slippers*) And these our daddy is going to have. With tulips on, which I myself have embroidered—I detest tulips, of course, but he wants tulips on everything."

MARIE *"looks up from the magazine ironically, curiously."*

SCHIWE

(*Cautious, doubting*) This is a *good* play, isn't it?

STRINDBERG

It is good! (*Hurt*) A classic, if only it gets performed sometime.

But this dribbling at the mouth . . . this female shit . . . We aren't getting anywhere! It would help if at least *someone* kept his mouth shut sometime!

SIRI
May we continue, maestro?

STRINDBERG
Yes!

SCHIWE
(*Anxious*) Naturally, I did not intend to express any doubt about the quality of the play, only . . .

STRINDBERG
Don't squeeze anything out! Hold it in!

SIRI
"(*Puts a hand in each slipper*) You see what small feet Bob has! Oh! And you should see how elegantly he walks. You have never seen him in slippers, have you?"

MARIE *laughs aloud.*

SIRI
"And then too, when he is mad, you see, he stamps his feet like this: What! Those damned maids—they can never learn to make coffee! Ugh! Now the cretins have not trimmed the wicks of the lamps properly. And then there is a draft on the floor, and his feet get cold: Usch, it is cold and those stubborn idiots don't know how to keep a fire in the stove! (*She rubs the sole of one slipper on the other*)"

MARIE *laughs, truly amused, perhaps a little high from the beer.* SCHIWE, *too, is amused.* SIRI *does an impressive characterization of* STRINDBERG, *his little fat hips, his prancing walk, his slightly feminine movements. Both women enjoy these little mime scenes immensely.*

STRINDBERG

(*Brooding, hurt, insulted*) You are playing it all wrong here! These are small moving details in the man which the wife describes with warmth! No ridicule here! The two women are fighting for the absent man's love; he is the center of the play! Warmth!

SIRI

Yes, darling. "Then he will come home and search for his slippers, which Marie has put under the dresser . . . But it is terrible to joke about one's husband this way. He is kind anyway, a good little man—you should have such a . . ." (SIRI *explodes suddenly into giggles.* MARIE *has difficulty repressing her laughter*) . . . Excuse me, I'll begin again . . . "He is kind anyway, a *little* man . . ." (*New laughter.* SIRI *begins with small discreet gestures of her little finger to give anatomical illustrations*) . . . My little man . . . oh, excuse me . . . excuse me.

SCHIWE

(*Irritated, but also amused. Red in the face, but looking back and forth curiously from* STRINDBERG *to the women*) Ladies . . . please, ladies . . .

SIRI

. . . a little man, a skinny little worm . . . (*Begins to hum and sing a dirty song*) . . . Oh, like a moist little earthworm . . . He couldn't get the little thing up at all . . . because, because it was too small . . .

MARIE

(*Calming down, but still laughing*) But, Siri . . . now you must . . .

SCHIWE

Mrs. Strindberg . . .

STRINDBERG *puts the script slowly, carefully on the floor and stands silent, looking straight ahead. His face is tired and expressionless, but it twitches nervously. The two women gradually grow calm. Then everything is silent, painfully silent,* STRINDBERG *does not move.* SCHIWE *sways up and down on his feet, toe–heel, toe–heel. He looks nervously at* STRINDBERG, *at the women, at the ceiling.* STRINDBERG *remains quiet for a long time.*

STRINDBERG

Siri, you have promised so many times. (*Very softly, as if to himself*) Although I always knew that I could not trust you. That you would take advantage of every chance. Because you knew that it hurt. Every time, at a certain point, it came. Sometimes in the face, sometimes in the back. Only because you knew that I could not get over it. Could not sleep. It's unbelievable. You know that yourself. I adapted, as lovers always do, to your preferences. Played the page boy. The child. And everything else. Was gentle, let you . . . And then you spread the poison behind my back.

SIRI

Oh, there, little August. Don't take it so hard. You, too, must put up with some things.

STRINDBERG

Yes, I really must.

SIRI

It's that way for all of us. Our humanity is ground down and our feelings for ourselves are torn apart. It's the same for everyone. But you at least can always make literature out of it.

STRINDBERG

But not *because* of it. In spite of it. *In spite* of it. (*Low, as if to himself, in a growing rage*) And at the parties every night, among friends, always after she would get a load on . . . Then it would come. I was so simple. I was shy, discreet in my sexual activity. I thought she wanted it that way, loved me like a child. But despised me secretly. This last year now—love at forty—I have become cynical, raw, lewd, and she loves me like . . . like a man. Like a *man!* (*With great bitterness*) . . . So I am a man! Now she even takes a beating, as long as she gets what she wants. That's idealism!

SCHIWE

Mr. Strindberg . . . No one would take her few comments about . . . your size . . . other than as a joke . . . Doesn't mean a thing, Mr. Strindberg.

SIRI

Soon you will begin to tell how you screwed that seventeen-year-old Martha, too . . .

STRINDBERG

(*Furious*) You perhaps believe I laid that fiendish slut of my own free will!!!

SIRI

. . . well, uh . . . well, yeah . . .

STRINDBERG

And it came back and back and back again. Little pinpricks. My dearest mate smiled and joked and drank and then out it would come. Oh, little dear Siri . . . oh, that sweet little devilish swine . . . with those hazy, alcohol-drenched eyes and piquant little jokes . . . (*Roars*) As if it always were the screw's fault that the nut was too big!!! And everyone lapped it up . . . *Interesting!* . . . You remember Grez, Miss David! You cannot have forgotten! (*Pause*) The day after, enraged right down to my balls, I took the train to Geneva and took a doctor with me to a bordello. Strictly scientific. Controlled experiment. There I performed the feat of strength, for that matter not for the first time—what I would like to call Proserpine's abduction! Imagine the situation, Mr. Schiwe, like Bernini's statue! Freestanding group without support! Had my sperm tested. Was found to be fertile. Then it was measured, in erect condition. *Six inches by one and a half,* Mr. Schiwe! Six by one and a half! Scientifically controlled!

SCHIWE

(*Somewhat sheepish*) Six by one and a half.

STRINDBERG

(*Triumphant*) Exactly!

SCHIWE

Six by one and a half . . . Is one and a half inches the circumference?

STRINDBERG

(*Explosively*) Nitwit! Length 6, diameter 1½. That is the diameter!

SCHIWE

Oh yes, the diameter, oh yes . . . (*Seemingly brooding intensely*) I myself do not usually measure straight across . . . but perhaps one should do that, too . . . You are probably right there . . .

STRINDBERG

(*Interested and friendly*) The *circumference* is measured by taking the diameter, dividing by two, thus getting the radius, then working it out according to the formula 2π x r.

SCHIWE

Two π . . . r?

STRINDBERG

Two times π times the radius. π is equal to 3.14, that is a constant. The radius in this particular case is three fourths. The circumference, therefore, is 2 x 3.14 x ¾. The circumference is 4⅞ inches. That is the difference!

SCHIWE

Oh yes, of course . . . oh yes . . . that is a difference . . .

STRINDBERG

A *circumference* of one and a half inches would be this big. Like a lead pencil.

SCHIWE

Yes, of course, of course.

STRINDBERG

(*Factually*) My circumference is 4⅞ inches. I have measured it before.

SCHIWE

I trust you completely . . . trust you completely. (*Memorizing*) Two times π by the radius . . . 2 times π by the radius.

MARIE

My god, what are they doing?

STRINDBERG

Mathematics! (*Calmly*) Six by one and a half. Thus, opinion is built on false premises. (*Pause*) And still she continued . . . with her little implications. Her own infidelity (*stares darkly at her*)—with these talentless theatrical rogues and popeyed sons of bitches—that purely moral crime with all of its possible consequences—illegitimate children, syphilis—would naturally be forgiven because of my so-called weakness. (*He walks around the stage, in among the curtains, restless, his repressed bitterness and anxiety growing. Against the curtains of lions, savages with distorted bodies, and Indians, he seems very small, almost childishly frail*) I am supposed to be *weak!* I who traveled all of France in third-class, hiking with a pack on my back! In twenty-one days! Climbed the Alps, rode between Vevey and Lausanne and back! In twenty-four hours!! (*Now openly doubtful, tears of injustice in his eyes*) Swam in the summer across Vierwaldstättersjön, risking my life! Unbearably cold water, deadly agony! Rowed a boat back and forth between Kymmendö and Dalarö alone! And so on and so on! And I am supposed to be weak! Then why did I do all of that?

MARIE

Good question.

SCHIWE

You must calm yourself, Mr. Strindberg! Mr. Strindberg!

STRINDBERG

(*Sits, head in his hands, trembling*) I know . . . this is ridiculous. I must not *degrade* myself this way. There must be something else . . . I should not *need* to! It is peculiar . . . that these attacks on the man, the *cock* in me, are so painful. (*Pauses, rocks back and forth with the upper part of his body*) It is probably true. I was not so big . . . I am no *big* man in a calm state. But normal when erect! But that gossip . . . At last it became so important. I recall even during the period when I was writing *The Red Room,* I was taunted. (*With rising irony and distaste*) And held then in the presence of witnesses—a whore's, too— a cock examination behind the pub at the zoo. The whore—it was the one called the White Bear, besides—gave me a Pass, a Satisfactory, not, however, with Honors.

MARIE

(*Sympathetically*) Please, please. Stop now.

SCHIWE

(*During this whole time, has held out a pencil and paper*) Excuse me, that mathematical formula . . . 2 x π . . . Would you . . .

STRINDBERG

(*Angry, pointing at* SIRI *and* MARIE) It makes no difference! The women of the future will not need us! We will not be used! Just look at them. It is not only *my* prick they are indifferent to. Mr. Schiwe, *they are just as indifferent to your prick!* This applies to you, too! To all of us!

SCHIWE

(*Profoundly shaken*) But that cannot be . . . Mr. Strindberg, you cannot say *that* . . . (*throws his arms out, appealing to the women*) . . . that . . . you really cannot *say* a thing like that . . .

STRINDBERG

(*With energetic gestures*) Big prick! Little prick! Medium prick! Somewhat smaller than medium-big prick! *It makes no difference!!!* They have no use for us any more. (*Walks restlessly around* SCHIWE, *clenching and unclenching his hands*) I feel it. Something is happening! I feel it long before anyone else does! I have an alarm clock in my genitals! Bzzzzzzzzzzzzzzzzz! Something is happening! changing! Bzzzzzzzzzzzzzzzzz! Danger! Bzzzzzzzzzzz. Danger! Danger!

SIRI

. . . look at the man . . .

STRINDBERG

(*Angrily*) Maybe it involves you, too! Maybe you will be *left over,* too! (*Anxious, more confused*) All these new demands . . . these new female sex organs according to new research cannot be satisfied by just a cock . . . New, new . . . new rules . . . Do you know, Schiwe, everything is *tottering.* (*Shouts*) They call me revenge-hungry! Yes, I have no desire to be killed by women! Blow for blow, in self-defense! (*Cunningly*) And revenge suggests, even *proves,* that guilt exists! Guilt is punished, and punishment is a consequence! To punish someone innocent is irrational! Therefore, women are guilty!

MARIE

(*Moved*) Mr. Strindberg, I don't know anyone who so clearly demonstrates a woman's logic as you do. I have never met anyone, never read about anyone.

STRINDBERG

(*Reserved*) Women completely and totally lack logic.

MARIE

That's what I meant. But, besides, you express this "feminine" logic in such an interesting way. The lack of logic in you becomes . . . an aesthetic value.

STRINDBERG *glares sourly, exhausted.*

MARIE

(*Friendly and curious*) You have a fine little woman in you, Mr. Strindberg.

SCHIWE

(*Aroused*) "A fine little woman" . . . To call him that . . . How can you throw that in Mr. Strindberg's face!

MARIE

A soft, intense, and mysterious little woman whom you ceaselessly persecute and . . .

SCHIWE

No, now I must protest on Mr. Strindberg's behalf. Such filthiness . . . "Fine little woman" . . . He does not have to put up with that . . . That is . . .

STRINDBERG

I do not persecute. You do.

MARIE
Je? Who?

STRINDBERG
(*Very low*) You never allowed me to be the man I am. That is why I hate you so terribly. I mean: I hate them.

MARIE
Because . . . of that . . .

STRINDBERG
Precisely because of that.

MARIE
I can, from my own experience, perhaps understand what you . . . are trying to say.

STRINDBERG
Oh yes. (*Looks at her in silence*) Yes.

MARIE *rises, gets a beer, opens it.*

STRINDBERG
(*Neutrally*) The fourth.

MARIE
That's right.

STRINDBERG
You will drink yourself to death.

MARIE
Most likely.

STRINDBERG
Still, you live the life of a free person. Do you know . . . (*Looks shyly around, lowers his voice*) . . . If you promise not to spread it around . . .

MARIE
I promise. Say it.

STRINDBERG
I have a kind of sympathy for you. Respect. You don't only talk.
You have *done* something with your life.

MARIE
Thank you.

STRINDBERG
(*Interested and sincere*) Do you know that it is already 1889.
And these damned emancipation women have talked, decade
after decade, about women's liberation. But they don't *do* anything. Over half of the earth's population are women. But the
cowards have not freed themselves. History is full of examples
of oppressed men who have rebelled against the oppressors and
fought their way free. Women only talk. That is what drives
me crazy. I plunge into my work and I come up in six months
with two plays, a novel, and fifteen articles in my hand, and
those women are still talking. In the same salons. Have they
murdered any oppressors? Have they cut anyone's throat? Blown
up the prison? Organized riots? Is there blood on the walls?
No! The baboons chatter on! The day they *took* their freedom,
I would respect them!

MARIE
And stand on their side?

STRINDBERG
(*Completely amazed*) *Naturally* not! Fight them more than
ever! But with respect!

MARIE
Oh, that respect . . . that male egotism . . .

STRINDBERG
You are afraid of freedom, you know!

MARIE
Are we?

STRINDBERG
And if the baboons get their freedom, they drink themselves to death!

MARIE
(*Without any trace of suffering*) I am going to disappoint you. I don't at all think your views of women are so reactionary. But you have never understood . . . never seen . . . what prison . . . or freedom . . . really looks like.

STRINDBERG
Yes, yes, but the whining, the whining . . . that passive fucking talk! In a hundred years, all the men will have committed suicide in desperation over the whining . . . Thus, no more battle of the sexes . . .

MARIE
Actually, that is not very funny. (*Walks over and gets another bottle of beer, opens it*)

STRINDBERG
The fifth.

MARIE
That's right.

STRINDBERG
You are going to drink yourself to death.

MARIE
Most likely.

STRINDBERG
In a way, that would be a pity.

MARIE
You won't think so tomorrow.

STRINDBERG
Why did you begin, anyway?

MARIE
Well, it was not because of any damned freedom.

STRINDBERG
(*Cheering her up*) It's probably just a weakness of character. You were probably born with it. You have got bad blood. (*Looks curiously at her*) I've heard that they say that Georg Brandes . . . sometimes called *the great Brandes* . . . is supposedly your father. He was in your home when he was young, had a relationship with your mother, although she was married . . . Is that right?

MARIE
Brandes, that phony radical . . .

STRINDBERG
Aha! (*Cheers up a little*) You have literary judgment, anyway! But that must be where the character weakness comes from!

MARIE
Think, Mr. Strindberg. (*Reflectively*) If you had met my mother. An illegitimate child from the red-light district, raised like a plantation slave among Copenhagen's aristocracy. Oh, Mr. Strindberg, if sometime you would write about the *daughter* of a servant, instead of your own life as the son of one. But you won't.

STRINDBERG
(*Not listening, wanders around the room with his hands behind his back*) It's almost ghostly. Brandes's daughter, the plague's

infection in my house . . . I have always suspected that Brandes
. . . He writes somewhere about your mother . . . the "oppressed
woman," and how she gave him an insight into the "prison"
of the institution of the family . . . Isn't that right? Brandes,
the favorite of all of the women's leagues . . .

SIRI

(*From the bed in the background*) Now you have given him
grist for the mill. Conspiracies and women's leagues. Watch out
now.

STRINDBERG

Child of a viper. I knew it.

MARIE

(*A little tipsy*) Oh, the great Brandes. A fine, educated radical.
Very educated. (*Slightly ironic*) He had the right opinions about
everything, but what did that do for my mother? Yes, that was
her that he wrote about, he had never seen anyone like her. She
never gave in. It was so fantastically exotic, he thought, an oppressed child of nature, a bird . . . you know. A bird in her
cage . . . He was so taken by her . . . And at last he got her
to run away from the whole rotten thing. With me and my
brother, like a book, great literature. Although afterwards he was
stuck there with her, and then it got painful.

STRINDBERG

Theft of a wife. Brings with it pain . . . or torture . . .

MARIE

She probably believed that Brandes was *freedom* . . . that he
was her new life . . . that it was *possible* to fly. But really Brandes
was not in love with her. He only had a great *compassion* for
her . . . as beautiful as she was . . . so oppressed by her older
syphilitic husband . . . so tragic . . . It was, you know, great
literature! (*Reflectively*) She was truly beautiful. The most

beautiful slave on the whole plantation. (*With rising intensity*) But she did not *know* anything! She had never gotten to learn anything, only lived there like a decoration . . . and then when she fled, freedom itself was painful. She had not read any books . . . had not seen any plays . . . she had nothing to say . . . she could not just *run away* from prison. The prison came with her! And Mr. Brandes was such a well-educated humanist . . . with such compassion . . . for the *oppressed* . . . Although after my mother was free, freedom itself was *painful* . . . for everyone . . . So it did not work.

STRINDBERG
I assume that she drank herself to death.

MARIE
(*Deliberatively*) Sometimes, when I think of all the radical, well-educated, and prejudice-free humanists I have met, then I think it is really nice to talk with a son-of-a-bitch like you, Mr. Strindberg.

STRINDBERG
But Brandes was your father, then, anyway! And so the poor old man, the married man *betrayed by his wife* . . . was forced . . . forced to pay for your upkeep, to be ridiculed in Brandes's books, to raise illegitimate children, to support his parasite wife . . .

MARIE
Calm down, now, Mr. Strindberg. Brandes was not my father. The only thing my mother was uncertain of was whether my respectable, syphilitic, legal father's Wednesday or Friday rape was responsible for my birth. He had such decided habits, you see!

STRINDBERG
Like rats in a hole.

MARIE

I knew her most after she was . . . free. Freedom had become a perverse idea for her. She thought—an insane idea—that she was *not* a baboon with a criminal psyche continually ready to copulate. Such mad ideas kill women very quickly, Mr. Strindberg!

STRINDBERG

So.

MARIE

The thing that broke her, she once told me, was that in that freedom no *use* could be found for her. She was completely . . . Freedom was completely . . .

STRINDBERG

(*In a low voice*) . . . useless. I know.

MARIE

(*Scrutinizes him, still a little drunk*) You know? (*Pause*) You know, Mr. Strindberg? Do you know the night we had our little farewell dinner in Grez? (*Very matter-of fact*) You described it so nicely. What fine *words*. "Warm rain." "Damp night." And . . . "saw how the Danish monstrosity" . . . And then the end there with its fine "gray dawn," "tribades' night." But I wonder if you ever understood how I felt; to be kicked out with all the courteous forms like a useless rat. "While we held a farewell dinner for our friends." So incredibly *educated!*

STRINDBERG

Don't drink any more. (*Painful pause*) Yes, yes, I remember.

MARIE

You said that you drank the red-haired swine drunk. Yes, that is the way it was. Because around the morning hours suddenly all that immense *education* had drained and everything was awful

. . . awful . . . and honest. I remember that we found ourselves outside the house, down by the road. I was there. Siri was there. And so were you. Do you remember?!

STRINDBERG
Yes.

MARIE
Yes, you do.

STRINDBERG *moves in an ice-blue, hazy light, as though in a dream, while* MARIE *speaks.* SIRI *is with him. They move very slowly, scream and talk without making a sound, with white faces and opened mouths. The only thing one hears is* MARIE'*s words. It is an evil, slow dream; the music cuts softly but intensely under* MARIE'*s words;* STRINDBERG *and* SIRI *dance their slow, merciless ballet in the blue-white light around* MARIE, *who tells about the morning in Grez.*

MARIE
I was terribly sick. I lay with one arm against . . . it was probably the gatepost, and vomited. Vomit got on my dress. Oh god, I was sick. Siri ran around, around the road in meaningless circles and cried and screamed. Ran and cried and screamed. And I threw up on my dress. And Siri cried. It was like separating a pair of Siamese twins with a meat ax, did you know that? Did you know that?

STRINDBERG, *his face blue-white, his mouth gaping, his movements terrified and slow, moves around her, pointing at her, while* SIRI *moves in an outer circle.*

MARIE
You stood only a few yards from me. I was terribly drunk, but I saw your face and saw that your mouth was moving. Soundlessly. I think you screamed and swore at me. I heard nothing,

but you were probably yelling at me. I was terribly sick. Several children stood some distance away and stared . . . I think they were from the village. But I only saw your face. It was completely gray. Your mouth moved like a black hole. I didn't hear anything, anyway. And then, suddenly, all at once. Suddenly I liked you, I liked you tremendously.

STRINDBERG *freezes. The light is less blue, the movement ceases, his mouth closes, the music glides upward and dies. He opens his eyes and looks ahead emptily.*

MARIE
I thought I understood you completely. No one had meant to use the two of us. That was what was so terrible. It was as if that mad, pale-gray face with the black hole for a mouth (*rises, walks over to* STRINDBERG), *as if it was my face,* my face too.

STRINDBERG
(*Emptily*) Yes, yes.

MARIE
There must have been a terrible scandal in Grez.

STRINDBERG *remains silent, then suddenly touches her, shyly, with his hand.*

SCHIWE
(*Insecure, wishing to break the mood. Begins, hesitantly*) For my part, I look at woman as a flower . . .

STRINDBERG
What?

SCHIWE
Must we not . . . try . . . to experience the being of a woman like a plant . . .

STRINDBERG
(*Emptily*) Oh. Oh my god, is that idiot still . . .

SCHIWE
We are all also waiting for the photographer. He is supposed to come tonight, you know.

STRINDBERG
The photographer?

SCHIWE
He is supposed to immortalize you with the ensemble of the Dagmar Theater. For the future.

STRINDBERG
For the future. Yes, yes, that.

SCHIWE
Should I . . . find out . . . where he is?

STRINDBERG
Yes.

SCHIWE *exits*.

SIRI
(*Has lain on the bed, rises, comes forward*) We are getting nowhere. I assume that this is the end of my theater career.

STRINDBERG
The theater offers no consolation.

SIRI
Yes, but I cannot help it if I hoped for a comeback. (*Looks at* SCHIWE) God knows if he will even return.

MARIE
Is it finished, then?

STRINDBERG

(*Sits down, very tired but stubborn*) No, we must continue. We must pull ourselves together now. I have debts and we need the money, and I can't get loans anywhere. There is only one little escape hole: this experimental theater. No other theater will perform my work. No publisher will take my books, no one takes my articles, everyone talks shit about me. Ten years of persecution and they have me here. Down here. This wretched rathole. The Dagmar Theater, this damned play. That's what we have. We are not completely useless. So we must rehearse *The Stronger* to the end. It's as simple as that.

SIRI

So?

STRINDBERG

So. We. Continue.

MARIE

Yes.

STRINDBERG

(*Laboriously*) Page 5, at the top. "Our friendship was so curious."

SIRI

"Our friendship was so curious." (*Pauses, looks for a long time at* MARIE) Yes, really.

STRINDBERG

(*Friendly*) Oh, please continue.

SIRI

"Our friendship was so curious—when I saw you the first time, I was afraid of you, so afraid that I dared not let you out of sight; wherever I came or went, I always found myself near you—I dared not be your enemy, so I became your friend." (*Coldly*) Thoroughly ridiculous. (*Continues abruptly*) "But there was always disharmony when you came to our home, because I saw

that my husband could not stand you." That's true. He saw that
freedom is something that can infect. "And then I felt uncomfortable, like a dress that does not fit—and I did everything to
get him to be friendly to you, but did not succeed—until you got
engaged! Then you became great friends, so it looked for a while
as if you dared show your feelings only then, when you were
safe." Safe in prison, he means. Truly ingeniously reversed, I
must say. Was it supposed to be that poor Sofie, then, who was
the fiancée . . . and if she and Marie were together . . . then
you were less jealous . . . But that is the way it really was, my
dear. It was *you* who was jealous of . . .

STRINDBERG

(*Immensely irritated*) That damned commentary! That unbelievably *private* way of reading literature . . . this unbelievable
arrogance and egocentricity . . . As if it were *obvious* that it
concerned you and your damned apes . . . as if you were the
center of the world . . . Act, don't talk! Once and for all, you
must learn to act and keep your mouth shut!

SIRI

Should I let the words come out through my ears, then?

STRINDBERG

Act and shut up!

SIRI

Yes, but this is so unbelievably bad, truly false, besides; I see it
more and more when . . . when we ourselves do it. The only
chance for this play to succeed in Copenhagen is to play it in
Finnish and say that it is by Ibsen!

STRINDBERG

(*Furious, pointing angrily at her*) Ibsen! You! You! I will *silence*
you to death in my books in the future! That will be your punishment!

SIRI

Help. I'm dying. Can it be possible?

MARIE

But must we discuss what is true and false in reality when we give this *play*, it is so . . .

STRINDBERG

(*Points violently at the script*) True, every word! A pure documentary truth! Don't try and lie it away! A document! Wasn't there disharmony in the marriage, just as I have *concretely identified* and *documented* here, wasn't there disharmony in the marriage when this sow came? ? ?

SIRI

Dear little August. You are always, at all times, like so many other men, gripped by a totally irrational fear when you meet a free woman. Then the alarm clock rings in your balls. Bzzzzzzzzzz! Danger! Bzzzzzzzzzzzz! Then you get deathly afraid and scream that she is a lesbian. Bzzzzzzz . . .

STRINDBERG

What! Isn't she a lesbian, then? What!

MARIE

And if so: *so what?!!*

STRINDBERG

(*Passionately emphasizing each word*) It is not the *free* woman that I am afraid of. I can't stand anything but free women, you know that. But these free women should *work*, and *like me*, and not, on the other hand, talk shit and *disdain my cock!!!*

SIRI

For you, a woman is certainly not like a flower . . .

STRINDBERG

If she is, she should be a poppy. Beautiful to look at, and opium on the inside. Opium! Irresistible when one begins to try it, and addictive. Intoxicating and addictive. (*Delighted with his fine image*) A woman is like a poppy!

SIRI

Oh, that hatred of women . . . I don't understand it . . .

STRINDBERG

Oh, that incredible *bullshit* about my hatred of women. (*With great pathos and self-pity*) I have nothing, absolutely nothing against women. (*Points accusingly*) But would you, would you want your daughter to marry one?!!

SIRI

Oh my god, yes, what a relief.

MARIE

But what kind of a world is this . . . what is it . . . when someone like you . . . when a man like you has to stand here and scream and measure lengths and diameters and be afraid and look at us as if we were a narcotic and . . .

STRINDBERG

(*Does not listen, is suddenly all alone in his voice like a child*) Siri, I know, you are disappearing, this is the last night in our lives. I will never see the children again; I know that you will be merciless; I won't see Karin . . . Greta . . . Putte. So it is, Siri. And I know that I must either die or live on. *And I can only live if I have a woman.* That's the terrible part. I'll go to Ohrwall at the children's hospital. He will get me a young woman who has just had a child. The father unknown, vanished. She should be a young woman, she does not have to be pretty. A girl about twenty-five, with hips and breasts. I'll take care of her and raise her child, sleep with her and give her new ones. I must have children, for without children crying I can't live.

SIRI
So he thinks.

STRINDBERG
Do you think I'm alone in that?

SIRI
No, it is precisely that. New slaves to oppress. We oppressed women have . . .

STRINDBERG
We oppressed! *We!* What damned we? For hundreds of years the Swedish peasant woman has been working, working on the farm, but besides she has run the home's finances and economy, decided her children's education, been the religious authority in the home, decided very nearly *everything!* While the man has slaved away at his work and subordinated himself. That is the reality for the majority of women, Miss von Essen! And then comes this fiendish noblewoman from Finland, who has not done a day's work in her life, and tells us about the *oppressed!* You have no *right!* Not even to talk about the truly oppressed. If my mother were here (*now nearly in tears*)— that fine, *quiet,* patient, charming, and oppressed hard-working woman—she would chew your ass out!! Calmly, without an unnecessary word!

MARIE
That doesn't make sense, Mr. Strindberg. Your logic is feminine.

STRINDBERG
(*Roars*) But my intuition is *superior* to yours! I can *smell* a truth miles away! Sniff it out! *Retrieve* it!

SIRI
(*Walking restlessly back and forth*) In contrast to both of you . . . I am not amused by any of this. I've heard it too many

times. These retrieved truths. That noble, quiet, dead mother. That silent . . .

STRINDBERG

(*Starts to attack her*) *Touch* her! If you touch her! *Touch her holy memory!* If you even try . . .

SIRI

Don't touch me. Jesus. Oh no, then. I am thinking of only *one* thing. Will I on the ninth of March 1889 get to make my come-back at the Dagmar Theater or not?

MARIE

Siri's right.

STRINDBERG

Yes, yes, for once. It is late, we are tired, but it is true. We must actually try to be ready. We must . . . concentrate . . . take the hardest part. Page 8, perhaps. Page 8. The long hate mono-logue, when she understands that her friend once tried to take her husband away from her.

A moment of tense silence.

SIRI

Well, well, will wonders never cease. Wonders never cease. Did I get it right that time?

STRINDBERG

(*Pretends not to understand*) That is the script! You must re-spect the script! The script says that the two women find them-selves in a battle over the same man. The absent man still is in the middle of the action. They both love the absent man and fight for him. That is the *script!*

SIRI

Yes, darling. We love him. Passionately. Do I get to kiss a picture of him now and then? It would certainly . . .

STRINDBERG

Page 8 at the top. "That was why."

SIRI

Okay, Marie. Okay, we rehearse again.

STRINDBERG

"That was why." Damn it, begin!

MARIE *hangs tiredly over the bedpost at the end of the bed, and* SIRI *sits gently beside her. She begins calmly, almost resigned, to read against the words;* SIRI's *voice is warm, intimate, almost caressing.*

SIRI

"That was why I had to embroider tulips which I hate on his slippers, because you like tulips, that was why." (*Takes* MARIE's *hand, caresses it softly*) "That was why we were supposed to live by Mälaren in the summer, because you could not stand the Baltic Sea; that was why my son was supposed to be called Eskil, because that was your father's name; that was why I had to wear bright colors, read your authors, eat your favorite foods, drink your drinks—your chocolate, for example; that was why —oh my god—it is dreadful." (*Very warm, softly, with a little smile*) "It is dreadful when I think of it; it is dreadful . . ."

STRINDBERG

(*At a loss what to do, pleading*) But, Siri, you are reading it completely wrong. You are not supposed to have that tone. Siri, it should be with hate! With hate! You must act it with hate!

SIRI

(*Does not appear to have heard*) "Everything, everything came from you to me. Even your passions. Your soul crept into mine like a worm into an apple, and ate and ate until only the peel was left, with only a little black mold inside." (*Now abandoning herself more, she caresses* MARIE) "I wanted to fly from you but

I couldn't; you lay like a snake and enchanted me with your black eyes—I felt my wings lift, only to be pulled back down; I lay in the water with my feet tied together, and the more I tried to swim with my hands, the deeper I sank, down, down, until finally I sank to the bottom, and you lay there like a giant crab ready to take me in your claws—and now I am lying there." (*With a great sense of calmness, softly*) "Oh, how I hate you, hate you, hate you."

STRINDBERG
(*Has let the script fall to the floor, stands quite still and rocks in the middle of the floor, says with a childish, thin voice*) Siri. It is not supposed to be played that way . . . That is not the meaning . . . Siri . . .

SIRI *has let her script fall, holds tightly and desperately on to* MARIE, *caressing her. They embrace one another more and more heatedly. Suddenly* SIRI *begins to cry. She cries desperately, unrestrainedly. She presses her head against* MARIE's *breasts, caresses her, cries sobbingly, yet still happily.*

SIRI
Oh, Marie, Marie. I have been so alone.

MARIE
(*Closes her eyes, holds* SIRI *in her arms as if she were a child, rocks her back and forth to quiet her*) Little Siri. Dear little Siri. Cry. You can cry now. It is over now.

STRINDBERG *walks with very small steps to the chair and sits. His face is gray and empty, it twitches, he looks out toward the audience. He is silent. The bed, where the two women are, lies in half darkness, their bodies half visible; the only sounds that are heard are* SIRI's *gradually diminishing sobs.* STRINDBERG *remains silent. The music is very low.*

MARIE

(*She frees herself from* SIRI, *walks across the stage, toward* STRINDBERG. *She pulls up a chair, sits right beside him. She speaks very calmly, very kindly, to him*) Mr. Strindberg.

STRINDBERG

(*Does not answer, but his upper body rocks almost imperceptibly back and forth. From between his closed lips comes an almost inaudible moaning, or a song on one note*) M m m m m m m m m m m m m m m m m m m m m m m m m m m m m m m m m m m m m m m m m m m m m m m m m m m m m m m m m m m m m . . .

MARIE

Mr. Strindberg.

STRINDBERG

M m m m m m m m m m m m m m m m m m m m m m m m m m m m m m m m m m m m m m m . . .

MARIE

Mr. Strindberg, you have not written a very clear play.

STRINDBERG

(*Stops abruptly, waits, then in a barely audible voice*) I know.

MARIE

Yes, yes, of course you know.

STRINDBERG

I knew—after that night—that it was all lost. Then I wanted to write a play about how it should be—when we met again.

MARIE

After the operation with the meat ax.

STRINDBERG

Yes.

MARIE
And so you wrote a play about two women who loved an absent
man and . . .

STRINDBERG
Exactly that . . .

MARIE
Although you knew that . . .

STRINDBERG
I knew that everything was lost. I still wrote it the way I wanted
it to be.

MARIE
As you *wanted?*

STRINDBERG
Sometimes you must write things the way you *want them to be.*
You never know. It might have helped.

MARIE *looks carefully at him, does not answer.*

STRINDBERG
(*Almost childishly surprised*) I feel completely empty. Completely weightless. As if I were only a thin shell. Empty.

MARIE
Mr. Strindberg, what you wrote about marriage—it seemed so
true to me. And you yourself were the truest man I had ever
met. Yet you lied constantly . . . One could never really believe . . .

STRINDBERG
If you throw two rats into a pit, Miss David, they cry. Then
they become cannibals. So it is. I am crying. Pick me up out of the
pit, Miss David.

MARIE
Yes, I understand.

STRINDBERG
No, no, you don't. I loved the pit, too.

MARIE *says nothing.*

STRINDBERG
It was the same for Siri and me as for most people. We thought
we owned each other, and lived our lives and resented one another. If we had been more generous, perhaps it would have
gone better.

MARIE
(*Nods, hesitates, says cautiously*) You understand probably that
. . . in the future Siri and I will live together.

STRINDBERG
(*Long silence*) Yes. I understand.

MARIE
May I confess one more thing?

STRINDBERG
Yes?

MARIE
I do not think all that badly of you.

STRINDBERG
Thanks. (*Silent a moment*) Thanks, and the same for me. (*Very
simply and cordially*) I assume that you realize that, in the
future, I will be forced to fight you.

MARIE
That is obvious.

STRINDBERG

(*Just as friendly*) That with every means I have at hand I must pursue you like an enemy. Must persecute you, slander, fight. I am obliged to do that, you understand.

MARIE

I understand it. I accept it, too.

STRINDBERG

(*Softly touches her hand*) That is the way it must be.

MARIE

I know. That is our condition.

THE PHOTOGRAPHER

(*Comes in quietly through the door, unnoticed. Stands there motionless with his apparatus under his arm, tripod, camera, cloth, box. Looks around, and says without surprise*) Is this where I'm supposed to be?

SIRI

(*She has been lying curled up on the bed in the background. Now rises, completely calm. She straightens her hair, straightens her dress, which has gotten wrinkled, buttons a button on the waist*) Yes. This is it. Get ready.

STRINDBERG

(*Rises, goes toward the proscenium, says calmly and directly to the audience*) After the night's rehearsal at the Dagmar Theater in Copenhagen in March 1889, it was all over. *The Stronger,* with Siri von Essen in the one role, had its première on the ninth of March, and was a fiasco. It was performed only once. Strindberg returned to Sweden, and the divorce was a fact. Siri von Essen and Marie David moved in together, lived first in Sweden, then in Finland, where Marie died after a few years, of tuberculosis. However, Strindberg met Marie Caroline David one more time. It happened by accident, in Lerkila, on the twenty-fourth of June 1891. But they did not have time to say a single word, since Strindberg in a burst of violent rage immediately attacked Marie and knocked her down some stairs. He did not hurt her seriously, and in the ensuing trial Strindberg was fined a total of 135 Swedish crowns. That was the last meeting between them. After that, he never saw her again.

THE PHOTOGRAPHER
(*During this time he has quietly and efficiently mounted his camera equipment*) I am ready now.

SIRI *walks toward* STRINDBERG, *takes him by the arm. He follows obediently like a well-trained dog, walks in rhythm with her. She leads him with one arm,* MARIE *is at her other arm. They walk to their places in front of the camera.*

THE PHOTOGRAPHER
The gentleman should stand in the middle.

They position him correctly. STRINDBERG *stands now in the middle. On his left side stands* SIRI. *She leans softly and affectionately against his shoulder. On the other side is* MARIE. *She stands with lowered head, slightly turned away, as if in deep thought or as if she does not want to be part of the group.*

STRINDBERG *is in the middle, straight and completely still. He stares directly ahead.*

Then a brilliant magnesium flash: an ice-blue cloud that makes their faces deathly pale. At the same moment the stage goes dark; the picture that is taken is projected greatly enlarged against the background and the music plays very loud.

--◆{ TRANSLATOR'S NOTES }◆--

page 3. With Enquist's agreement, the McCarter Theatre production deleted the opening slides.

page 4. Siri's swearing in Finnish reflects her Finnish-Swedish background. Members of the Swedish upper class, such as Siri, who lived in Finland did not learn Finnish. The implication of the scene is that Siri learned to swear in Finnish but probably knows nothing more of the language. (Finnish differs completely from the other Scandinavian languages and is not understood by other Scandinavians.)

page 5. The phrase "Will wonders never stop" attempts to convey the sense of a cliché in Swedish which means, literally, "One hears a lot before one's ears fall off." In the original Swedish, Siri says "One sees a lot before one's ears fall off," and Strindberg corrects her. The phrase falls somewhere between the English "We live and learn" and "Will wonders never cease."

page 9. I have substituted "a pair of old shoes" for the Swedish "a pair of worn-out pants," since the effect of the cliché seems more important than the phrase itself.

page 10. In a number of specific cases, such as "mad enough to shit on the devil," I have elaborated a Swedish swearword or phrase in order to sustain the occasionally vulgar humor and vitality of the play.

page 11. *Tschandala* is a long short story written by Strindberg in 1888 in which gypsies are given a clearly inferior role.

page 13. *Miss Julie* had been banned from public presentation in Copenhagen in 1889.

page 15. The Swedish original also mentions Strindberg's play *Paria*.

I have deleted the name after *The Stronger,* since it would have no meaning for English-speaking audiences.

page 18. See introduction, p. xi, for an explanation of Grez.

page 20. Siri von Essen made her acting debut after she left her first husband and took up with Strindberg. In the first few years of their marriage, she pursued an acting career and he wrote roles for her. Eventually, however, his jealousy and his accusations of infidelity with members of both sexes prevented her from performing. The end of her career presumably led to the dissolution of what they had hoped would be a "partnership of artists."

page 25. The Princeton production quite legitimately interpreted the "subtle little dig" that Schiwe notices as Schiwe's realization of Strindberg's sarcasm toward him and his speech. In a purely literary context, the line is somewhat difficult to understand.

page 30. "I go. You go. We go" has been inserted by the translator to suggest Strindberg's play on words. Occasionally in *Tribades* Strindberg's use of words that are psychologically rather than logically related is difficult to understand. On the same page, Strindberg's outburst, apparently out of context, about the Swedish children's story alo reflects this use of psychological association.

page 36. In *The Son of a Servant,* Strindberg's father is described as cold, aloof, severe. Presumably, "Icelandic nature" is a reference to that.

page 42. Axel Lundegård was a writer and companion of Victoria Benedictsson, also a Swedish writer, who wrote under the name Ernst Ahlgren. She and Lundegård were active in the debates on sexual equality that raged through Europe in that period. Her suicide in 1888 is thought to be the basis of Strindberg's *Miss Julie.*

page 45. What is being quoted is, of course, *The Stronger.*

page 59. "The red-light district" is specifically referred to in the original as Dyben Street 185, but the reference is to the prostitution quarter of Copenhagen.

page 59. Marie is referring to Strindberg's major autobiographical novel *The Son of a Servant* (1886) when she expresses the wish that he would write about the daughter of a servant.

pages 59–60. Georg Brandes, the distinguished Danish critic and literary historian, author of the six-volume *Main Currents of Nineteenth-Century Literature*, was influential in getting Strindberg to go to Copenhagen to begin his experimental theater. Marie Caroline David was rumored to be the illegitimate daughter of Brandes, but, as far as is known, these rumors are unfounded.

page 64. During rehearsals, Enquist added stage directions to walk over to Strindberg, where Marie says "as if it was my face."

page 71. Strindberg's reference to "the long hate monologue, when she realizes that her friend once tried to take her husband away from her" implies that Marie may actually have tried to seduce Strindberg. Siri's understanding of this possibility explains the following lines.

page 77. Enquist deleted a few lines of the original play at this point during rehearsals. The deleted lines are as follows, after Marie says "I know. That is our condition":

STRINDBERG

(*Takes a deep breath. He is tired, stares straight ahead, looks next at Marie and runs his hands over his eyes*) We must finish the rehearsal.

MARIE

Yes.

STRINDBERG

We can't stop where we are. We must go on. We have so much left to do.

MARIE

And so much further, we have so much further to go.

page 77–8. As is true of several points in the play, Enquist has changed some of the actual facts given in the Strindberg speech, to suit his own dramatic purposes.